About the author

Pete Chrisp has worked as a writer and editor for newspapers, magazines and books since 1979. His books include the highly acclaimed *Riding Shotgun*, co-written with Rory Gallagher's bass player, Gerry McAvoy; the best-selling *The Chain: 50 Years of Fleetwood Mac*; and the recently published *The Beatles on Vinyl*. He has also edited myriad music books across a wide range of topics – from the Byrds and folk music through to tube amps and collectable guitars. He lives in Kent, England.

For their help, advice and encouragement, many thanks to
Gary O'Neill, Huw Thomas and Sally Beeby.

In memory of my proggy school friend and inspirational Genesis fan, Paul Carter.

Supper's Ready

More than 50 Years of

ESIS

Written By
Pete Chrisp

sona
BOOKS

© Danann Media Publishing Ltd 2022

First published in the UK 2022 by Sona Books an imprint of Danann Media Publishing Ltd

CAT NO: SON0496

Photography courtesy of

Getty images:

- Michael Putland
- Koh Hasebe/Shinko Music
- David Warner Ellis/Redferns
- Michael Ochs Archives
- Ian Dickson/Redferns
- John Lynn Kirk/Redferns
- Rick Diamond
- Angelo Deligio/Mondadori

- Paul Natkin
- Paul Harris
- Luciano Viti
- Lynn Goldsmith/Corbis/VCG
- Mick Hutson/Redferns
- Darryl James
- Graham Wood
- Caem/Hanekroot/Redferns

Alamy images:

- MediaPunch Inc
- Jeff Morgan 03

- Pictorial Press Ltd
- Alamy Posters

Other images **Wiki Commons**

Book layout & design Darren Grice at Ctrl-d
Additional proof read by Juliette O'Neill

Made in EU.
ISBN: 978-1-912918-59-1

A REVE

An introduction to Genesis

Anyone who's a big music fan knows all about the best-known phases of popular music that arrived from unique locations across the UK and USA and dominated the music scene: New Orleans jazz in the late 19th Century; Chicago Blues from the Twenties onwards; the Nashville Sound country-and-western from the mid-Fifties; the Mersey Sound that gave us the Beatles in the Sixties; the Canterbury Sound from the likes of Caravan and Soft Machine, elevating English baroque pop and jazz fusion into the charts in the Seventies; later that decade, the youth scenes in New York and London resulted in the New York Dolls and the Ramones, the Sex Pistols and the Clash, grabbing the music scene and shaking it by the throat; or Madchester in the Eighties producing the Stone Roses, Happy Mondays, acid house raves and, ultimately, Oasis. Great times for all lucky and young enough to take part and survive.

And then, of course, traversing the late Sixties all the way through to this decade's Twenty-Twenties, we have... the Surrey Sound. Not heard of it? Yes you have. Because the Surrey Sound, in a nutshell, is Genesis. Not punk rock. Not even prog-rock. But posh rock.

Genesis was created at a very expensive boarding school called Charterhouse in the early Sixties. They arrived on their first day, probably lonely and certainly homesick, but all bright, clever and sharing a love of music. As if by some act of God, they all met, got to know each other, play together, not kill each other, and combine their love of the Beatles and Stones, Motown and Stax, hymns and symphonic classical composers, with a bit of folk and jazz thrown in for good measure, to create something unique: Genesis. Quintessentially English music written in large country mansions by posh schoolboys. How lovely.

In reality Genesis became targets for criticism throughout their careers. Some regarded the band as overtly middle-class, drawing attention to and often ridiculing their wealthy parents and private education. As Peter Gabriel once described it: "To this day, we've never outgrown the snotty, rich-kid thing..."

In the Eighties they switched to more commercial soft-rock and pop and rose to a level of success far higher than the early days with Peter Gabriel and Steve Hackett, but were never loved or admired in quite the same way. Criticised by fans for 'selling out', it was a lose-lose situation – pompous, prog heavyweights in the Seventies, limpid, easy-listening lightweights in the Eighties and onwards.

To find anyone who likes all elements of Genesis equally is not easy, but increasingly – to which I add my own prog-influenced ears – there is much to admire in the later years. There are no bad albums as such, but some that leave fans frustrated as to what might have been... Instead, let's celebrate what was and remains some of the most interesting progressive rock and hit-making pop of the last 50+ years.

A little education can take you a long way and theirs certainly did. From Charterhouse in Surrey to playing across the world to over 25 million people, selling more than 150 million albums and, in 2010, being inducted into the Rock & Roll Hall of Fame as one of the most influential bands of their generation.

Deo Dante Dedi: God having given, I give. The Charterhouse school motto. Genesis have certainly given the world a great collection of wonderful music.

Pete Chrisp November 2021

Posh kids and public school prohibition

The English school system takes some understanding, even if you're English.

First, there are 'nursery schools'; those are for babies from about 10 minutes old to four or five for parents who need to earn a living to afford to pay the nursery fees. Then there are 'primary schools' from five to 11-year-olds, split into two groups – 'infants', for five to six-year-olds, and 'juniors', from seven to 11. Most importantly, they're free, unless, of course, your parents are posh, or rich, in which case you will probably be sent to a 'prep school', short for 'preparatory school' – a 'private school' where you prepare for 'secondary school'. Some prep schools, however, allow pupils to start from the age of about two up to 16 or even 18, so you won't need to prepare for a secondary school because you'll already be there. A prep school is 'private', or 'independent'. Not for the public. No, if you've been to a prep school, you'll probably go on to a 'public school'. Public schools take prep school pupils usually from the age of 13, but if you've stayed on at a prep school until you're 16 you might be able to move to a public school for your A-Levels. Unless, of course, you've proved yourself a bit thick, in which case you'll probably go to a local art college and just muck about for a couple of years.

A public school is another school that's private. It's not for the public either. If you're just a member of the public you'll go on to a 'state school' or, if you live in the right region, possibly a 'grammar school'. A grammar school is a state school for the public that tries to look like a public school (that's private) by having slightly posher buildings in slightly posher areas with slightly posher teachers and allow some of the slightly brighter pupils to be boarders (ie live there during term time) just like a public school, so they can all pretend they're at one. The only difference is that a grammar school is free because it's run by

the state and most of the students are day-pupils (unless you live there, in which case you're a boarder and your parents will have to pay for you to board), while a public school costs an arm and a leg, whether you live there or not. On average, your parents will be coughing up about £5,000 a term, or £15,000 a year for a day-pupil (where you go home each evening) or around £30,000 a year for a boarder (where you don't).

If you go to one of the best public schools in England, however, where you usually have to be a boarder, you'll be looking at a minimum of £15,000 per term – or between £40,000 to £50,000, per year. The best English public schools are Eton (where English Princes and politicians come from), Harrow (where foreign Princes and politicians come from), Benenden (where English and foreign Princesses come from), Gordonstoun (which is actually in Scotland but still qualifies, where English Princes and Scottish actors come from) and one called Charterhouse. Where Genesis come from. Simple. Charterhouse was established in Smithfield, central London, in 1611 originally intended to educate bright pupils from poor backgrounds, but was relocated to Godalming in Surrey in 1872 – probably because the headmaster at the time realised that parents down in Surrey had a lot more money than fathers who were meat porters at London's Smithfield Market and would have drunk most of their wages by 7.00am in pubs that opened at 4.00am. There are one or two London pubs that still open nice and early for market traders, or anyone else who fancies a pint at the crack of dawn.

Charterhouse is now ranked as one of the best, and most expensive, of the top seven English Public schools and it was here, from 1963-65, that no fewer than seven young men cast their eyes and ears on one another and would go on to form (or manage) one of the world's most successful bands of all time, eventually known as Genesis. Just as well for their parents, hopefully, in terms of getting back some of that investment money, because most, if not all of them, absolutely loathed

Charterhouse. It was, like most English public schools at that time, a Dickensian place of learning stuck in the 19th Century and run along draconian rules in a misguided effort to save the British Empire; "a fearsomely repressive institution" was how Peter Gabriel later described it.

Music was not encouraged at Charterhouse unless it happened to be religious, classical or choral. That proved a lucky break in many ways, because its influence on the Genesis symphonic sound would prove considerable. But pop music? No, no, no. If you were caught playing an electric guitar, for example, or listening to a Beatles album when you were meant to be doing your banco (homework), for example, you would have earned yourself a caning. That was another English public school tradition back in the Sixties – corporal punishment, along with 'fagging' (where the younger boys were forced to perform menial chores for the older ones), but it's probably best if we just move on.

The first lamb to the slaughter to enter Charterhouse's hallowed grounds was a 13-year-old boy called Anthony 'Tony' Banks from East Sussex, the son of a teacher, with an older brother who had also attended the same school, and also hated it. Their mother was a talented pianist and had encouraged Tony's enthusiasm and interest in music from a very early age. When he left home to attend the Boarzell prep school in Hurst Green at the age of seven, his mother arranged for his piano lessons to continue with the headmaster's wife. By the time he arrived at Charterhouse, he was already an accomplished pianist and at some stage had also taught himself to play guitar. By the end of the first day at Charterhouse he'd made a new best friend, a boy his own age who was also obsessed with music, by the name of Peter Gabriel.

Gabriel joined Charterhouse on the same day, in keeping with a family tradition, having been born and raised in a very musical family in nearby Chobham, Surrey. His father came from

a wealthy family of timber merchants but he was also lucky enough to have a mother who played the piano, introducing him to lessons at a very early age. Peter had gone to two different prep schools in the local area from the age of eight and at some point also learned to play the flute and the oboe and became somewhat obsessed with drums and percussion. He added a tom-tom to his musical arsenal by the age of 10. Once settled in at Charterhouse he joined a trad jazz band, called the Milords, as their drummer, and was also involved with another band during school holidays, the Spoken Word, with another Charterhouse pupil called Anthony Phillips.

The following year, in September 1964, another Surrey-born pupil from nearby Chertsey, Mike Rutherford, arrived at Charterhouse, although he had been brought up predominantly in Portsmouth on the south coast of England, where his father had been a senior Royal Navy officer. William Rutherford CBE DSO had risen to the rank of Captain of HMS *Suffolk* during World War II and gone on to become Commanding Officer of Whale Island in Portsmouth Harbour in 1955. He retired from the Royal Navy soon after and moved to new employment in Cheshire, where Mike eventually attended the Leas in Hoylake prep school from the age of seven.

There was no great musical history in the Rutherford family, but his parents had noted his early interest by the age of eight and arranged guitar lessons for him. At the age of 10 he started his first band, the Chesters, with his drumming school friend, Dimitri Griliopoulis, and various other boys who couldn't actually play anything. Mike's parents were considerate enough to take him to Manchester in 1963 to watch Cliff Richard and the Shadows perform at the Apollo. It was from that day on, having stared in awe for two hours at Hank Marvin's red Fender Stratocaster, that any chance of Mike Rutherford following in his father's footsteps in the Royal Navy sank without a trace. He hated Charterhouse probably more than any of the other Genesis boys and became known within the school as something of a rebel. Over his four years there he had got used to being caned on a regular basis, often by his housemaster, Mr Chare, who seemed to consider Rutherford, with his longish hair and thrashing an electric guitar, something akin to the antichrist.

Following Mike, one year later, the second of several Anthonys with a prominent role in the Genesis story - this one being Phillips, luckily known to his friends as Ant rather than Tony - had made his way to Charterhouse after leaving the St Edmund's prep school in Hindhead, Surrey. The son of a very successful and wealthy merchant banker, Ant had shown real potential for music even while at St Edmund's. At an early age he had already taken up guitar and piano and formed a band, called the Spiders, with another talented young boy blessed with one of the best rock 'n' roll names of all time, Rivers Job. Rivers was older than Ant and transferred to Charterhouse a year before him; when Ant arrived in April 1965, they continued their musical friendship and, within a short space of time, formed a band together called, initially, the Scarlet and the Black, but later changed to Anon.

Although Ant's transfer to Charterhouse had been relatively painless because he already knew his older friend, Rivers, and fitted in more comfortably because he was pretty good at cricket, it was music, he said, that "was the only thing that could obliterate the feeling of sheer misery and uselessness". The Beatles were his and the other boys' saviours, along with the Rolling Stones, the Kinks, the Small Faces, the Who, the Yardbirds, John Mayall and, particularly for Peter Gabriel and Tony Banks, black soul singers such as Nina Simone, Otis Redding and just about anyone else signed to Stax and Motown Records.

Anon was made up initially of Mike Rutherford on rhythm guitar, Ant Phillips on lead guitar, Rivers Job on bass, Rob Tyrell on drums and a boy called Richard Macphail who, having wanted to be the drummer but not deemed good enough, revealed his talent for mimicking Mick Jagger; as most of their set was made up of Rolling Stones covers, he was the perfect man for the job. By this stage Tony Banks and Peter Gabriel had also formed their own band, Garden Wall - a jazzy outfit very different to Anon, which included a trumpeter called Johnny Trapman and

on drums, a new boy called Chris Stewart (apparently having been taught how to play by Gabriel). They were older than the Anon boys and, being in a different school house to the others (until Ant Phillips and Chris Stewart arrived), the two bands were not particularly close to each other. Arguments still rage as to which was the better of these rival bands, but all are agreed that the most talented musicians among them at that stage were Rivers Job and youngest member, Ant Phillips.

Richard Macphail, however, was not given an opportunity to progress with his music career due to his equally draconian parents deciding he had fallen in with the wrong crowd (they were convinced he should become a church minister) and therefore be moved to a more appropriate public school - Millfield in Somerset, renowned for its sporting prowess. Determined to leave with a bang, however, Richard demonstrated his future skills in the arena of music management and promotion by organising, against the school's wishes, a Charity Beat Concert at which Garden Wall, Anon and a new band called Climax would perform - the Battle of the Bands, Charterhouse style. Mike Rutherford had formed Climax when he and Ant Phillips fell out after Ant rather cruelly ridiculed Mike's musical talent. Rutherford was replaced by another Charterhouse boy, a music scholar called Mick Colman.

Despite the beady eyes of the headmaster and various other fun-quashing teachers patrolling the school hall during the afternoon Beat Concert, the event went well and was also the first occasion on which four future Genesis members played together. Garden Wall didn't possess a guitarist or bass player; Ant Phillips and Rivers Job happily stood in for them before their own set with Anon and, thus, for the first time, Gabriel, Banks, Phillips and Stewart took to the stage together.

It was Anon, however, that stole the show, with Phillips, Job, Tyrell, Macphail and Colman bashing out Rolling Stones numbers as if their lives depended on it. For Richard Macphail, sadly, and for Rivers Job, it was their Charterhouse swansong. In the summer of '66, Macphail moved on to Millfield while Job (due to some sort of discipline issue) left school after taking his O-Levels. He did, however, achieve his ambition of becoming a professional musician when he joined the English blues band Savoy Brown and played on two of their albums, *Getting to the*

Point and *Blues Matter*. (Tragically, Rivers was killed in 1979, at the age of 29, when he was struck by a train in London.)

With Anon now needing both a vocalist and bass player, Rutherford was invited to rejoin Anon. He didn't have a great voice but his move to bass proved a wise one; in truth, his guitar playing at that stage had never been too impressive, either. "I'd only learned about three chords a year since I was eight," he later claimed. "By the time Ant arrived, that was still the case!" It was also decided that, despite his musical talent, Mick Colman didn't quite fit the bill and he was asked to leave.

What is so remarkable about the development of Genesis at Charterhouse is that, being a school where any music that was obviously not classical, or a hymn, or something by Charterhouse alumni such as Vaughn Williams, would be so rigidly frowned upon by the powers that be, how the boys managed to find the time and places where they could get together regularly to practise without being caught, thrashed or possibly shot. As Peter Gabriel once described their situation, Charterhouse was "Colditz in the middle of suburbia".

Rutherford even had his guitar confiscated by his nemesis, Mr Chare, but was more determined than ever to carry on, whatever the punishment might be. He was eventually expelled from Charterhouse at Chare's insistence, but it was Mike's father, Captain Rutherford, who spoke to the headmaster and had Mike's ejection delayed until he had at least had the opportunity to sit his O-Levels. Mike retained his huge respect for his father but simply did not want to be like him. His rebellion continued to such a level that, having heard of successful runaways at other public schools such as Eton and Harrow, he had bought himself a motorbike and, in the style of Steve McQueen's performance in *The Great Escape*, would regularly sneak out at night to do such dreadful things as go to the pub, meet his girlfriend, or even drive to London and watch bands play at the Marquee in Soho. The difference, unlike other runaways, was that he would return to his prison camp every night. "Even while I was busy rebelling it seemed paramount not to embarrass my father," he said, rather touchingly, in his 2014 memoir *The Living Years*.

For all of them, the Genesis musical journey had proved far

from easy; it was not a case of four, humorous, mop-topped Liverpudlians getting together in their hometown and writing music that would change the world; or five, rebellious, rather scary-looking Londoners who would thrill young girls while frightening their parents; these were a group of posh, privileged, young boys who had been thrust, unwillingly, into an antiquated upper-class education system they despised and, despite their shyness and insecurity, had stuck to their ultimate desire to write and perform music totally different to anything else at that time.

Ironic, then, that their big break arrived in the shape of a former pupil called Jonathan King (possibly the only one who claims to have actually loved his years at Charterhouse!) who paid a visit to the school in 1967 to present awards at the annual old boys' reunion. King had left Charterhouse in 1962 with the intention of studying English at Trinity College, Cambridge, after a gap year travelling the world In an attempt to make contact with various music industry luminaries (including the Beatles' manager Brian Epstein, whom he met in Hawaii in 1964) to fulfill his ambition of becoming a pop star and record producer. Once at Cambridge he joined a band called the Bumblies as lead vocalist and concentrated on writing his own material to sell to various performers. After several attempts but little interest, he eventually recorded one of his own numbers for Decca Records, entitled 'Everyone's Gone to the Moon', which made it to No. 4 in the UK charts in August '65. It went on to be recorded by one of Peter Gabriel and Tony Bank's great loves, Nina Simone. By September '65, King had formed his own record company, Jonjo Music, with his business partner and music publisher, Joe Roncoroni, based in Soho Square, London.

By late '66, Ant Phillips and Mike Rutherford were friends again and had started writing music together. By the Spring of '67 they had enough material to record a demo tape of five tracks at a small studio in Chiswick, set up in his attic by another Charterhouse friend, an electrical whizz-kid called Brian Roberts. With Phillips on guitar and Rutherford on bass, they decided their songs would benefit from the addition of a piano player and invited Tony Banks to join them. Banks agreed on the proviso that he could record a song he and Gabriel had written together, called 'She is Beautiful'. In fact, he suggested,

Peter is a much better singer than either of you two, and can play drums, so why doesn't he come along as well? The deal was done, the songs recorded; now all they had to do was somehow get the tape to Jonathan King.

Being something of a superstar to the Charterhouse wannabes, they were too shy to approach him with their tape cassette when he arrived for the old boys' reunion, but persuaded a friend called John Alexander to hand it over to him (or possibly just leave it on the seat of his car – as always, when it comes to music memoirs, there are varying versions of exactly what happened). To everyone's amazement, he played the tape and was hugely impressed, especially with Peter Gabriel's voice. Within a few days he had called the telephone number on the cassette and invited the boys to pay a visit to his flat in London.

From summer to autumn of 1967, at the ages of just 15 to 17 (and with a record producer who was still only 22) they paid two visits to Regent Sounds Studio in Denmark Street (London's rather shoddy equivalent to New York's Tin Pan Alley) and recorded two more demo tapes. Jonathan King was not particularly impressed with them but still managed to get them a deal at Decca Records to record their first two singles – 'Silent Sun' and 'A Winter's Tale' released in February and May 1968. They were decent Sixties baroque songs that sounded suspiciously like the Bee Gees (King was a big fan), but both failed to chart.

On drums they had brought along Chris Stewart from Peter and Tony's Garden Wall but, the truth was, he wasn't very experienced as a drummer. King had spotted that immediately and told the rest of the band they needed to find a replacement. (King hadn't been overly impressed by Rutherford's bass playing, either, but the others refused to consider replacing him.) In Chris's place came Jonathan 'John' Silver, another public schoolboy from St Edward's in Oxford, who had become friends with Peter Gabriel at an Oxbridge tutoring college in central London which they were both attending. The band's slightly more impressive third single 'Where the Sour Turns to Sweet' (released in June 1969) was recorded at their third visit to Regent Sounds in the summer of '68 as part of the sessions to record their first album.

The problems with all of these releases, of course, was that, despite many arguments among the band, no-one as yet had come up with an acceptable name to print on the disc. Anon was no good, and nor was Garden Gate or Climax, so it was left to Jonathan King to come up with an answer. Some of their music, he decided, had a rather religious feel to it, so how about Gabriel's Angels? No one was too keen on that (apart from Peter Gabriel), so King's second option was a name based on where, according to the Bible, it all began: Genesis? Why not? And their first album would be called *From Genesis to Revelation*. All sounds great. Except the album was released in March 1969 in a plain brown cover with gold lettering, but no images of the band or even their name. When it was finally delivered to the record stores, staff thought it was a religious LP, and racked it accordingly. That might explain why it sold only 649 copies.

But Genesis had arrived. Hallelujah.

Carshalton College of Further Education
Students' Union

are presenting

GENISIS

and

JODY GRIND

at the College
NIGHTINGALE ROAD, CARSHALTON

on

SATURDAY 20th JUNE

from 7.30 p.m.

Admission : S.U. members 8 shillings
Guests 10 shillings

A giant leap of faith at Christmas Cottage

here's no doubt that Jonathan King's involvement with Genesis, although brief, was very important in that he provided them with their first recording experience and boosted their confidence in believing they could make it. But it had been very clear from the outset that their time with him would be limited.

The initial contract he had offered the boys had not been generous (in keeping with the music industry in those days) but, still being minors, it was up to their parents to approve it. Having wisely taken advice from a music business lawyer they were able to improve the deal and reduce the length of time King and Decca would be in control of the band down to just one year. When the time was up, it seemed that King, unimpressed by the album's sales figures, just sort of lost interest and allowed the boys to depart in control of their own destiny. (Mike Rutherford, however, remembers it slightly differently: they told him they'd split up, but then reformed within a few weeks once the dust had settled.)

The band members were grateful to King for the opportunity he had given them, but none were too impressed by his production on *From Genesis to Revelation*. Although there were some decent songs on the album, King had drowned just about everything with strings or brass overdubs, completely against the sort of sound Genesis were searching for. Now they were free to make their own decisions, the first one being, were they going to carry on?

Being younger, Ant Phillips was still at Charterhouse doing his A-Levels while Rutherford had made the move to Farnborough College to finish his education and was considering a career in journalism. The older members, Gabriel, Banks and Silver, however, were now all at the age when university beckons. Tony had already decided to go to Sussex University to study Chemistry; Peter had been offered a place at the London School of Film Technique and was considering a career in movies, either as a director or actor - he'd already auditioned

and been shortlisted for a role in Lindsay Anderson's superb film, *If*, portraying, ironically, a revolution that takes place at an English public school, but in the end decided to make music his priority; John Silver, however, had been persuaded by his parents not to give up his education for the flimsy chance that he would make it in the music business. He'd already been offered a place to study Leisure Management at the Cornell University in New York State, USA, and it proved too enticing.

After band discussions, the decision was made to give it another go for a year by attempting to go professional and give themselves every chance of success. Once again, although concerned about their boys' futures, their very supportive parents gave them every assistance they could, not least of which contributing £150 each to help the boys buy some new equipment including a Hammond organ for Banks. They also allowed the band to rehearse in their houses while on holidays or away for weekends, but it proved difficult having to switch regularly from one house to another; what they needed was a permanent rehearsal location. It was at around that time that Rich Macphail made a return to the fold and, once again, demonstrated his organisation skills that would eventually see him become the band's roadie and, eventually, tour manager. Rich had left Millfield School and spent some time at a kibbutz in Israel 'getting his head together, man', as one does at that age. Having made contact with the band and hearing about their need for a permanent rehearsal room, he came up with the idea of using his parents' Christmas Cottage in Wotton, near Dorking, Surrey. It might have proved more difficult to persuade them if it hadn't recently been broken into, leaving his mother feeling nervous about staying there again.

The decision had been made to sell the cottage in the Spring when the weather improved, which meant it would be sitting empty for the next six months, possibly more. The idea of it being looked after by the band (despite them being the 'wrong crowd' that resulted in Rich leaving Charterhouse for

Millfield) was better than allowing thieves and ragamuffins to run wild and trash the place. In addition, Rich's father, who worked for the food company Rank Hovis McDougall, managed to get them an old bread van for band transport, even though it was only capable of 45mph. Their only travel options up to that point had been their parents' smelly old horseboxes and an old London black cab that Peter Gabriel had purchased.

The next problem to solve was finding a new drummer to take John Silver's place and, as always through an advert, they managed to track down John Mayhew, a former carpenter from Ipswich but now a professional drummer who, being at least three years older than the others, had considerable experience of playing on the London pub and university circuit. Once set up in Christmas Cottage, so began their industrious and dedicated period of six months writing songs and rehearsing for up to 10 hours a day before, eventually, using their slow but sure bread van to begin gigging up and down the country. John Mayhew also made use of his carpentry skills to improve comfort in their bread van by making and fitting a partition wall and some new bench seats. Luxury.

Along with a friend of Ant's called Dave Rootes who came in as their roadie, the seven boys all lived together at Christmas Cottage with, as always, Richard Macphail keeping everything running smoothly, even cooking their meals, making bread and putting together picnic hampers – not, as everyone tends to assume, because they were so wealthy, but because they were so hard-up. It was cheaper for Rich to buy local produce and put together a picnic rather than having to stop for meals on motorways at inflated prices. He was also the one who would act as the peacemaker to deal with Charterhouse-style arguments that would break out almost every day. "Without Rich," said Mike Rutherford, "I think we would have killed each other."

In such a close, sealed off environment, clashes and flashpoints were inevitable and could be sparked off by even the most trivial of issues, not helped by their inability, thanks to the baggage that came with a Charterhouse upbringing, to communicate with one another in a pleasant manner. Instead they would shout, throw tantrums and storm off for an hour before skulking back into the rehearsal room. Nothing would be said. No praise or positive emotions were ever put on display. The intensity, at times, was unbearable. "We were too young to realise that you need room to breathe," said Ant Phillips. "Gradually things started to fall apart because, although the relentless hours of practice were very important, it wasn't great for our personal relationships."

Years later, having been a comparably sane grammar school boy, Steve Hackett once told them that, in his opinion, their lives had all been "fucked up by public school", and they agreed with him! "I think it robbed them of a childhood," said Hackett. But their resultant public school arrogance – plus a decent education that encouraged their interest in literature, history, reading, and even religious music – also helped them to evolve and survive in a difficult environment.

It was here at Christmas Cottage that Genesis' follow up album *Trespass* was written during their six months of self-isolation, and it's easy to hear the influences they had soaked up during that period. On the rare occasions that they had some time off, they would search for inspiration by listening to other young bands such as Family from Leicester, Londoners Fairport Convention, and endlessly to King Crimson's first album, *In the Court of the Crimson King*, which had a huge impact on the Genesis sound. Says Tony Banks: "We loved the sound of the Mellotron, the whole grandeur of the music, which was something we'd been trying to do, taking the early Moody Blues and developing it one stage further."

During any other free time, Peter Gabriel, with help from Rich Macphail, would spend hours on the phone chasing work by ringing venues and booking agents such as Terry King, a leading London promoter who started to get them local gigs in the Capital's venues, importantly including the Marquee. This was a big improvement over their early bookings such as their first official gig at a private birthday party near Charterhouse, earning £25. Their first proper gig was at Brunel University in January 1970; such was their inexperience that they didn't even know how to set up their equipment properly and Ant Phillip's guitar was completely out of tune, which wasn't good for his level of confidence.

Gigs followed at Twickenham College, a hotel in Kingston, Woolwich Polytechnic and a works event for a company in Smethwick, near Birmingham, for a crowd that wanted to dance around their handbags to the latest hits. Not ideal, nor was the next night at a youth club in Stockport, Manchester, so far from home that they had to spend the night in a freezing cold squat in Buxton, Derbyshire. Having had the dent to his self-esteem at the Brunel University gig, Ant was also suffering from health issues. After being diagnosed with glandular fever six months earlier, he was finding the stress and physical demands of being on the road hard to cope with, regularly ending up sick in bed seemingly every few weeks.

A more positive development occurred in early January 1970 when the band were asked to work with BBC producer Paul Samwell-Smith (previously the bass player for the Yardbirds) to put together a soundtrack for a TV documentary based on the life and works of the British artist, Mick Jackson. Samwell-Smith was impressed by a tape he had heard of the band and, although the songs were never used by the BBC, they did eventually end up as new material that evolved into numbers

on *Trespass*. (the 'Jackson Tapes' can be heard on the bonus disc of the *Genesis 1970-1975* boxset.) A month later, Genesis paid a visit to another BBC studio in Maida Vale to appear on the radio show 'Night Ride', performing six new songs including 'Looking for Someone', 'Stagnation' and 'Dusk'. Their contact with Paul Samwell-Smith also saw Peter Gabriel being invited to a studio session to play his flute on Cat Stevens's third album, *Mona Bone Jakon*. It's not something Gabriel particularly likes to remember; being so nervous, his quivering lips and heavy breathing could clearly be heard on the recording, much to the amusement of the other more experienced musicians.

With Terry King's support, and another promoter called Marcus Bicknell (who had considered managing them at one stage), bookings started to improve thanks to lots of support gigs with bands such as T. Rex, Caravan, Deep Purple, Johnny Winter, Barclay James Harvest and Mott the Hoople; they were even asked to support David Bowie and his new band called Hype at the Atomic Sunrise Festival at the Roundhouse in London on 11 March 1970. Suddenly, things were starting to move up a gear. Bowie's theatrical performance and outrageous costumes definitely had an effect on Peter Gabriel and it was at this time he began telling the audience short but rather bizarre stories to cover how long it was taking Mike, Ant and Tony to tune their 12-string guitars. It was better, he'd decided, to do something on stage rather than just stare at the audience silently.

It was at the Marquee on 19 February 1970 that Terry King got them a gig supporting a lesser known but very talented progressive rock band called Rare Bird, with whom they became good friends. Rare Bird's record producer, John Anthony, was also at the gig and was sufficiently impressed by Genesis to give them details on Rare Bird's independent record company, Charisma. Recently formed in 1969 by a man called Tony Stratton Smith (known to everyone as Strat) – a former sports journalist who had gone on to manage bands such as the Nice, the Bonzo Dog Doo-Dah Band and Van Der Graaf Generator. All were now signed to Charisma along with Rare Bird and the Newcastle folk-rock band, Lindisfarne. Rare Bird's keyboard player Graham Field also called in at Charisma Records and recommended Genesis to Strat's assistant, Gail Colson, and her brother Glen, the company's press officer.

It was through Paul Conroy (a booking agent for Charisma who went on to become President of Chrysalis and Virgin Records) that Genesis were engaged on 3 March to play Upstairs at Ronnie Scott's, the smaller stage at the world-famous jazz club, just 200 yards from Jonathan King's Jonjo office in Soho Square and not much further from Charisma's offices in Old Compton Street. So impressed was the venue that Genesis was offered a Tuesday night residency for the next six weeks. Although the audience wasn't huge by any description, numbers started to increase as the word spread. Rare Bird's producer John Anthony also managed one evening to drag Strat out of his drinking club (a musician's hang-out called Le Chasse in Wardour Street) to Ronnie Scott's to have a look.

There had already been some limited interest in Genesis from Island Records, Chrysalis, Threshold and Warner Bros. but nothing had ever been followed through. Strat, however, despite the lack of numbers in the audience at Ronnie Scott's, recognised their talent and potential and offered them a record deal almost immediately. Genesis could not have been in any better hands. Charisma Records had been created by Strat to support interesting new bands and entertainers such as

Monty Python and Vivian Stanshall, and even the poet Sir John Betjeman – performers who didn't fit into any established category. Tony was a genuine music lover who could offer a level of trust and patience that would give all of his artists time to develop with the luxury of sufficient financial backing – £10 a week each for Genesis (about £200 in current money). Not a huge amount, but it made a big difference.

Once signed up, Strat also paid for them to stay at the Angel Inn in Godalming (near Charterhouse) for two weeks in May to select and rehearse material to include on their second LP, *Trespass*. Recorded during June and July and produced by John Anthony at Trident Studios in London, the new album demonstrated remarkable progress and improvement since *From Genesis to Revelation*. It was impossible to make any comparison with their debut album, and hard to fathom how, after just 22 months, a band of schoolboys had managed to produce something as good as *Trespass*. The answer, according to Mike Rutherford, was simple: "We'd been playing *Trespass* live for so long before we went into the studio and as a result it felt like performing, not creating."

Disappointingly, the album sold in the region of just 6000 copies, but the potential was there for all to see and hear. Their third album (*Nursery Cryme*) was not much more than a year away; if Genesis continued to develop as impressively and at such a pace, the anticipation of what might come next was palpable.

Unfortunately, two more band members would have to fall by the wayside before such ambitions could be realised.

SUNRISE

at the

ROUNDHOUSE, Chalk Farm

SEVEN NIGHTS OF CELEBRATION
LIVING THEATRE ENVIRONMENT
GROUPS LIGHTS THEATRE

7 p.m.-midnight. Admission 10/-

MON., MAR. 9
QUINTESSENCE, GYPSY, BLACK SABBATH

TUES., MAR. 10
MARSHA HUNT, AUDIENCE, ALEXIS KORNER

WED., MAR. 11
DAVID BOWIE, GENESIS

THURS., MAR. 12
GRAHAM BOND, CLARK HUTCHINSON BAND JUICY LUCY

FRI., MAR. 13
BRIAN AUGER, FORMERLY FAT HARRY, HAWKWIND

SAT., MAR. 14
THIRD EAR BAND, LIVERPOOL SCENE, KEVIN AYERS & THE WHOLE WORLD

SUN., MAR. 15
ARTHUR BROWN, MIGHTY BABY, JACKIE LOMAX + HEAVY JELLY, PETER STRAKER & HAIR BAND PRINCIPAL EDWARDS MAGIC THEATRE

Many more Groups unconfirmed at Press Date — stay tuned
SURPRISE GUESTS
Advance tickets at the Roundhouse from Wed., March 4

FISHMONGERS ARMS
HIGH ROAD, WOOD GREEN, N.22

Tube: Wood Green Stn.
Buses: 123, 243, 29
141, 221, 298 and W4

Friday, October 9th, 8 p.m.
STRAY
plus HEAVEN

Tuesday, October 13th, 7.30 p.m.
GENESIS
plus TRAPEZE

All enquiries: 01-445 4228

JOHN'S SCENE LIGHTS   PLUS SONIC SOUNDS

CENTRAL HALL - CHATHAM HIGH STREET
Asgard present in concert

Saturday, March 28th
BLODWYN PIG   with MORNING

Saturday, April 4th
LIVERPOOL SCENE   with MR. CHARLEY

Saturday, April 11th
DEEP PURPLE   with GENESIS

Tickets 10/-, 14/-, 17/-, 20/- (send S.A.E.) from Central Hall Box Office, High Street, Chatham, Kent, Medway 43930, or at door on night. Doors open 7 p.m.

BRIGHTON DOME
PROGRESSIVE PROMOTIONS present
in concert
TYRANNOSAURUS REX
RARE BIRD
GENESIS
WEDNESDAY, FEB. 18th, 8 p.m.
Tickets: 15/-, 12/6 and 10/-
Dome Box Office - Brighton 682127

John & Tony Smith in association with Tony Stratton Smith
and Terry King
PRESENT
TOGETHER IN CONCERT
on the following dates

January 24th Lyceum Strand London *
   "   25th Town Hall Birmingham
   "   26th Colston Hall Bristol
   "   27th City Hall Sheffield
   "   28th St. Georges Hall Bradford
   "   30th Free Trade Hall Manchester
   "   31st City Hall Newcastle
February 11th Dome Brighton
   "   13th Winter Gardens Bournemouth

VAN DER GRAAF GENERATOR

'Van der Graaf's 'The Least We Can Do Is Wave To Each
Other' was one of the best debut albums — any, one of the best
albums — of 1970, but their new epic 'H to He, Who Am The
Only One' threatens to overshadow it to a large extent'
RICHARD WILLIAMS, 'MELODY MAKER' 28.11.70.

LINDISFARNE

'Herald an exciting new band — one of the few to have
emerged this year... Their hallmark is strong, clear,
straight-ahead songs... Alan Hall and Rod Clements reveal
a simplicity and force-fulness of approach reminiscent
of Lennon and McCartney in their mid-period'
MICHAEL WATTS, 'MELODY MAKER' 12.12.70.

GENESIS

'This is exactly what Genisis required to compile the
beautiful 'Trespass' — The time and patience to
achieve perfection... Now, without doubt, they have
come of age. At the famous Mothers Club, they are
regarded as the best new band to have appeared there'
JEREMY GILBERT, 'SOUNDS' 9.1.71.

ADMISSION ALL SEATS 6/- (30np)

Numbered tickets available in advance from the box office
Admission 9/- this concert only

---

*CARSHALTON COLLEGE OF FURTHER EDUCATION
STUDENTS' UNION presents*

GENISIS

and

JODY GRIND

*at the college, Nightingale Road, Carshalton,
on Saturday, 20th June 1970 at 7.30
Tickets: S.U. 8s Guests 10s*

RIGHT OF ADMISSION RESERVED

FiiC PROGRESSION
AT THE SUSSEX HALL, HAWYWARDS HEATH
Saturday 18th July, 1970

GENESIS

Plus

IRON PROPHET

with heavy disco and lights,
9 till 12 – 7/-

FREE TRADE HALL (Peter Street) MANCHESTER

JOHN and TONY SMITH in association with
TONY STRATTON-SMITH present

VAN DER GRAFF GENERATOR

LINDISFARNE

GENESIS

SAT., 30th JANUARY, 1971, at 7-30 p.m.

IN CONCERT

CENTRE CIRCLE - - 6/-

F 19

Hatches, matches and dispatches

he saddest aspect of the story of Genesis is that, after two years of hard work and the first sign of a light at the end of the tunnel, Ant Phillips, the band member recognised by all as being the one who had put this band together and was the most talented musician among them, decided he couldn't carry on. He'd been feeling increasingly unhappy due to health issues caused by glandular fever some months earlier, that had led to bronchial pneumonia, not helped by his unhealthy lifestyle on the road. There were the ubiquitous 'musical differences' between he and some of his bandmates concerning songwriting, but the most important issue was his increasingly gripping stage fright.

What had caused the problem? There had been one particular night during a gig in Watford on 14 March 1970, supporting Atomic Rooster, when he was playing the introduction to a song and realised he had no idea what came next. Not a huge problem – something that affects most musicians from time to time – but for Ant the same thing happened again the next night, and started to occur more frequently. In the end, he was turning down his guitar so that no one could hear the mistakes he was now anticipating, and his levels of stress and anxiety continued to increase each day. "I was 17 at the time and had never confronted anything like this before in my life. I absolutely dreaded going out on stage."

When his bronchial pneumonia developed the following month, with understandable concern and pressure from his parents, he saw a doctor who advised him that the touring lifestyle was just not suitable for him in his frail condition of health and he should leave. With the recording of *Trespass* just around the corner, he went through the motions almost on auto pilot and then, at a gig at Richmond Rugby Club, he announced his intention to leave the band. His last gig with Genesis was at the King's Arms in Hayward's Heath on 18 July 1970.

It also proved to be the last Genesis gig for drummer John Mayhew as well; after several days of fretting over whether or not the band should continue without Ant, the decision was made to give it another go but, if they needed another guitarist, they may as well look for a replacement drummer as well. All were agreed that, despite being a decent drummer, John lacked sufficient energy and creativity and had problems finding an appropriate style of playing to suit their complicated music with its difficult drum patterns. There was also a feeling among the band that there was a problem as a result of their differing social backgrounds – a former carpenter, the son of a painter and decorator from Ipswich, mixing with four former Charterhouse public schoolboys...

Mayhew later said he never felt any awkwardness. "I didn't see them as toffs; they were just four guys." However: "I realised I didn't have the technical skills to carry me onwards and upwards. I think even at the time of recording *Trespass* I knew I'd be leaving soon, but I was still not looking forward to that moment: I had really grown to love the band's music." It's a great shame that two musicians who had contributed so much to *Trespass* weren't able to continue – who knows how things would have developed if they had; instead, an ad was placed in the trustworthy *Melody Maker* newspaper to find two new musicians that would fit the bill:

"Tony Stratton Smith is looking for 12-string guitarist who can also play lead; plus drummer sensitive to acoustic music."

Acoustic music. Hmmm. There happened to be a young man who, as always, had strolled down to his local newsagent on a Thursday morning, looking for work, to pick up his copy of *Melody Maker* and all the other music papers. He'd been playing in a few bands – such as the Real Thing (while still at Chiswick Grammar School), then an outfit called the Charge, followed by the Freehold. A bigger break came with the opportunity to join the touring band for John Walker (of the Walker Brothers), which went on to become a group called Hickory, with his best friend Ronnie Caryl on guitar. They finally changed their name to the much cooler-sounding Flaming Youth, and went on to record a much anticipated album called *Ark 2*. Which went nowhere. Phil Collins was out of work and looking for a band.

Certainly he was not a shirker when it came to hard work; born in Chiswick, west London, his father a London Assurance insurance broker who had high-hopes that his son would follow him into the insurance business (as he had followed his), Phil, however, had set himself an artistic and considerably higher target. Leaving Chiswick County Grammar at the age of 14, he'd switched to a stage school set up by Barbara Speake where his mother, June, worked as a theatrical agent. From an early age Phil had been taking part in adverts for the likes of Smith's crisps as a dancer, as a male model for knitting patterns and, most impressively, landing a juvenile lead role as the Artful Dodger in Lionel Bart's musical *Oliver!* in London's West End. (The role was shared with a young boy called David Jones who would go on to become the singer of the world's first manufactured boy band, the Monkees.) Phil also had minor roles in major films such as the Beatles' *A Hard Day's Night* and Ian Fleming's *Chitty Chitty Bang Bang*; his career as an actor looked promising until, as happens, his voice broke and he was no longer required. Not that it mattered: he'd decided from the age of about five that he wanted to be a drummer boy.

Influenced by Bill Bruford (then of Yes), and great jazz players such as Buddy Rich and two top ex-Miles Davis drummers, Tony Williams and Billy Cobham, Phil had set out on his chosen career full of passion and confidence (stages holding no fear for him) and had already auditioned (unsuccessfully) for bands such as Vinegar Joe, the jazz-rock band Manfred Mann Chapter Three, and even played a studio session for George Harrison on his classic *All Things Must Pass* triple-album at the age of 17.

As another face regularly to be seen at the Marquee in Wardour Street, Phil knew Tony Stratton Smith quite well and

let him know the next time their paths crossed that he'd be interested in the job with Genesis, thinking it might open the door for him; Strat, however, told him he'd have to apply and audition just like everyone else. Phil arranged for himself and Flaming Youth's guitarist Ronnie Caryl to make a trip down to Surrey along with all the other hopefuls. They arrived at Peter Gabriel's parents' house nice and early and were told by Mrs Gabriel that they could use the pool if they liked, while they waited for their turn. Phil dived straight in and made use of the time to listen to other drummers trying to make sense of the complicated Genesis drum patterns; by the time it was his turn to take the seat, he'd already worked out what he had to play. As Peter Gabriel said: "I knew when Phil sat down on the kit, before he'd played a note, that this was the guy who really was in command of what he was doing, because he was so confident."

Needless to say, Phil was offered the job (Ronnie Caryl, however, although a talented guitarist, was considered too bluesy to suit Genesis) and rehearsals got underway at the Maltings in Farnham where, yet again, Rich Macphail would demonstrate his commitment to the band by sleeping at the venue overnight to ensure nothing was stolen. Initially they worked as a four-piece band with Tony Banks taking care of the lead breaks on his keyboards, but it was soon clear that they had to find a replacement guitarist.

Since April 1970 Genesis had been playing fairly regularly at a venue known as the Friars Club in Aylesbury, Buckinghamshire, and became good friends with the important promoter there called David Stopps, a big supporter of the band. Stopps recommended a local guitarist called Mick Barnard who had played with a band from Aylesbury called the Farm. Mick was offered the job and rehearsals continued at the Maltings for almost a month until gigs with the new line-up got underway in October 1970. Mick performed with Genesis for over 30 gigs and one BBC TV performance on *Disco 2* (a precursor of *Old Grey Whistle Test*) recorded in November 1970. Once again, Barnard was a

Steve Hackett, Peter Gabriel and Phil
Collins performing in London, 1971

very capable guitarist who contributed considerable input into the band's preparations for the recording of *Nursery Cryme,* but it was felt that he just didn't quite fit the bill. Unbeknown to Mick, the search for a replacement continued and Ronnie Caryl was given a second audition and did play one or two shows with the band but just wasn't quite what they were looking for. In the end it was Peter Gabriel who spotted an advert in *Melody Maker* that sounded kind of interesting:

"Imaginative Guitarist/writer seeks involvement with receptive musicians, determined to strive beyond existing stagnant music forms."

The ad had been placed (one of many over the years) by a 20-year-old guitarist called Steve Hackett - a former Sloane Grammar School boy in London's affluent Chelsea district who had spent much of the last eight years in his bedroom perfecting his guitar technique. Eventually he had joined a band called Quiet World with his brother, flautist John Hackett, and recorded an album called *The Road* on Dawn records, a subsidiary of Pye, with reasonable success. Gabriel

called Hackett and an audition (of such) took place at Steve's parents' flat near Pimlico, Victoria, with his brother John joining him to perform a mix of classical, jazz and slightly weird stuff to represent his love of King Crimson, opera and J.S. Bach. How could he not be perfect? The band liked him and he was invited to come to see them play at the Lyceum in London. He liked them as well, and the deal was done.

Mick Barnard performed his last gig with the band early in January 1971 and Hackett joined them for his first gig on 14 January at University College, London. It was to a small audience, which was probably just as well as Hackett had technical problems with his fuzz box, which threw him off completely, and Collins had managed to get drunk and kept missing his drums. Steve must have been thinking: have I done the right thing here?

With his lack of experience of live performance it was not an easy introduction to Genesis for Hackett when, within two weeks of joining, Tony Stratton Smith came up with the idea of what became known as the 'Six Bob Tour' - a series of

GENESIS are playing at the New Lord Lee, Civic Centre, Gravesend on 16th.

NEW LORD LEE

Civic Centre, Gravesend
Thursday, September 16th, 8 p.m.

GENESIS

DANIEL'S BAND – HARD FAST & GREASY

Adv. 45p. Door 50p. Licensed Bar
Thurs., Sept. 23: KEITH CHRISTMAS + LORD LEE

gigs around the UK with label mates Van Der Graaf Generator and Lindisfarne. The intention, with tickets at just six shillings, was to encourage younger, hard-up fans to come along and see three of the Charisma acts perform on the same show. It proved to be a great success with many shows sold out, establishing all three bands as major UK acts.

Soon after the 'Six Bob Tour', Genesis headed over to Belgium for their first overseas gigs at La Ferme Cinq in the Woluwe-Saint-Lambert region of Brussels, followed by a live performance on Belgian TV – again all sell-out shows. A couple of weeks later the band performed 'Musical Box' and 'Stagnation' on Bob Harris's BBC radio show.

Confidence was growing and spreading through the whole band, especially Peter Gabriel, but it didn't help him when, performing once again at one of their favourite venues, the Friars in Aylesbury, Peter got carried away and jumped off the stage to discover he couldn't actually fly, and broke his ankle. He had to perform for the next few weeks, including the 11th Jazz and Blues Festival (Reading) in June, in a wheelchair, giving him plenty of time to think about stage presence and ways of looking more exciting.

For Tony Stratton Smith it was time to make a decision as to whether he should retain Genesis on his successful Chrysalis label. Enthusiastic, as always, he dispatched the band to his old home, Luxford House, near Tunbridge Wells in Kent, to write new material for the upcoming album *Nursery Cryme*, but with the clear indication that there'd be no further investment and things needed to improve. With John Anthony producing and David Hentschel as sound engineer, the recording took place over three weeks at Trident Sudios in London once again, and was released in November. Although not a great improvement on *Trespass*, if at all, *Nursery Cryme* was a good album and, for all of Strat's bluster, his label didn't provide anywhere near enough promotion when it was released, resulting in disappointing sales. The album peaked at No. 39 in the UK charts. It did, however, reach No. 4 in Italy.

Strat decided to keep them on the books, but it was clear something big needed to happen very soon or their days at Charisma, or indeed for the label as a whole, were numbered. Thankfully, in the distance could be heard the faint sound of a huntsman's horn calling the pack to join the chase. *Foxtrot* was on the horizon. Tally-ho.

MAIN IMAGE:
Phil Collins, London, 1971

The thrill of the chase

Genesis did their very best in early 1972 to improve their standing in Charisma, playing gig after gig in the UK, recording TV shows for the BBC's Sounds of the Seventies, plus similar TV shows and a festival in Belgium, followed by more rehearsals at the Maltings and as many more UK gigs as they could find. No one could accuse them of not working hard, especially Peter Gabriel in his attempts to come up with something new that would swing the band's recognition and gain them a more positive response.

One good sign was that their sales in Europe were good and increasing, particularly in Belgium and Italy, which had become saviours in terms of keeping the band and Tony Stratton Smith happier. An Italian tour during April 1972 saw them performing to large, enthusiastic crowds, including 20,000 fans at the Palazzetto dello Sport in Rome. As Mike Rutherford said: "England was slow, it was uphill, and suddenly we could go to a country where we were actually a bit more popular."

It was Gabriel, of course, in May of '72, who came up with a simple but effective turning point for their performance at the four-day Great Western Express Festival at Bardney, near Lincoln, at which Genesis formed part of one of the greatest UK festival line-ups ever: the Beach Boys, the Faces, Buddy Miles, Joe Cocker, Sha Na Na, Status Quo, Humble Pie, Vinegar Joe, Stone the Crows, Rory Gallagher, Wishbone Ash, Don McLean, Budgie, Nazareth, Jackson Heights, Lindisfarne, Focus, Atomic Rooster, the Strawbs, Monty Python, Spencer Davis and the debut performance of Roxy Music, among others. Peter's answer to stand out among such Seventies rock luminaries was to wear black eye make-up and a garish, heavy-jewelled, Egyptian collar around his neck and, most importantly, shave the top of his head to form a sort of inverted V-shape that made him look a little like the village idiot. Weird or not, it was very effective in front of their biggest UK audience to date, who seemed to love it. So did the media who were curious as to why he'd done it. "It's the result of a very nasty shaving accident," replied Gabriel. Dressing up, he realised, can win a lot of attention.

In front of 50,000 wet, bedraggled and slightly bemused fans, many of whom hadn't seen anything quite like Genesis before, the band performed 'Watcher of the Skies' live for the first time. They didn't go down a storm, exactly, but they certainly garnered considerable interest. This, obviously, was the right time to release a new album. Strat gave the band three months to come up with new material and organised rehearsal locations in Blackheath, southeast London, and in Shepherd's Bush, to the west of the city, where they could use an area beneath the Una Billings School of Dance, owned by a friend of Phil Collins's mother. Once again, John Anthony initially took the helm as producer but, following disagreements with the band over the production of a single, 'Happy the Man', earlier in the year, he was replaced initially by a producer called Bob Potter, who'd produced the successful *Fog on the Tyne* album from Charisma's Lindisfarne. It was soon clear, however, that prog-rock was not Bob's cup of tea and he was subsequently replaced by two new names: co-producer Dave Hitchcock (who'd worked previously with the Kent prog-rock band, Caravan) and sound engineer John Burns. For the first time, the band were also credited as co-producers.

Recorded during August and September 1972, the band played at Reading Festival and took in another short tour in Italy before concentrating on laying down new material and two popular songs they had been playing live for some time – 'Watcher of the Skies' and 'Can-Utility and the Coastliners'. Both are excellent numbers which, along with 'Get 'Em Out by Friday' would have stood out on any other Genesis album but, as elements of *Foxtrot*, are overshadowed by the superb, 23-minute example of Genesis genius, 'Supper's Ready'. It was primarily because of that number across almost all of the second side that the album achieved such acclaim and commendation in the British (and European) media, climbing to No. 12 in the UK charts and, as expected, to No. 1 in Italy. As soon as *Foxtrot* was completed, Genesis began promoting the album at the usual UK venues including the Friars in Aylesbury and London's Marquee before heading over to Dublin for a concert at the National Stadium on 28 September

– an evening that's remembered for a rather bizarre but brilliant piece of stage creativity from Peter Gabriel. As the band got underway on the extended instrumental section of 'The Musical Box', Gabriel snuck off to the side of the stage and, to the surprise of everyone, including the band, reappeared wearing his wife's rather nice, long, red, Ossie Clark dress and an enormous fox's head that he'd had made specially for the event. It had been Charisma's booking agent Paul Conroy who had come up with the idea of someone wearing a fox's head, but he hadn't meant Peter Gabriel! And *Foxtrot* wasn't even released for another week.

Remember, this was Dublin in the early Seventies – renowned for its besuited Irish showbands rather than an open-minded celebration of transgender rockers. Mouths fell open. Women fainted... Not really – they actually seemed to quite like it and, as a publicity stunt it did the job. Genesis appeared on the front cover of *Melody Maker* a few days later, just in time for a two-month tour across England, Scotland and Wales. That was the UK and Ireland sorted. Next came America.

Their first trip to the USA at the beginning of December 1972 wasn't really a tour at all, just a quick visit for two shows in Waltham, near Boston, and New York. The first show at Brandels University was a warm-up gig that went horribly wrong due to technical problems. Despite the fact that Rich Macphail had travelled over to the States a week earlier to ensure everything would run smoothly, he hadn't taken into account the USA's differing power supplies to Europe, which meant Tony Banks's organ was completely out of tune. Two nights later at the Philharmonic Hall in New York they struggled with similar problems plus the fact that Leonard Bernstein's orchestra was rehearsing in the afternoon, leaving the band with less than four hours to set up their gear and carry out a very basic soundcheck just 30 minutes before the doors opened. A classic case of rabbits in the headlights, the band were running in all directions, panicking and furious, resulting in Rutherford flinging his expensive Rickenbacker bass guitar into the lift that would take them back to their changing room. It was, as far as the band were concerned, a disaster, but Tony Stratton Smith walked in and told them that he, and the audience, thought it was wonderful.

The band returned home for Christmas before another busy period of gigs across Europe and the UK, and it was at the Rainbow Theatre in London's Finsbury Park that another turning point gig took place, on 9 February 1973. A couple of people had attempted to manage Genesis by this stage – a promoter called Marcus Bicknell for a short period followed by a Charterhouse old boy called Adrian Selby who went on to become their lighting designer. It was Adrian who came up with the idea of hiding all of the stage gear behind a white gauze curtain with a UV lights shining onto it, creating a rather mystical atmosphere on stage. The band opened with some dry ice and the dramatic Mellotron intro for 'Watcher of the Skies', followed by Peter Gabriel appearing from nowhere wearing Day-Glo make-up around his eyes and his latest black cape and batwing costume. The whole set-up cost not much more than £100 but was spookily effective and the audience loved it.

By this time Peter had increased the amount of storytelling taking place between songs and created a number of characters, wearing an impressive collection of outfits. It included an old man mask for 'The Musical Box', and, during the relevant sections of 'Supper's Ready' a flower headpiece for use during 'Willow Farm' and a six-sided fluorescent headpiece and heavy black cloak for use during 'Apocalypse in 9/8', beneath which was a white lame suit in which he would (on occasions, depending on the suitability of the venue) rise into the skies on a stage wire and float around in *Spinal Tap* fashion. Gabriel's wardrobe continued to evolve and, as always, the band never knew any more than the audience as to what would come next. Not all of the band were keen on these theatrical 'gimmicks', especially Phil Collins who felt Gabriel was winning all of the praise and media attention while the band got on with the important matter of performing the music.

There was one important question to consider: the band was about to embark on its first major US tour spending a month performing at colleges and small theatres across most of the East Coast and Midwest US cities, plus three shows in Canada's Quebec and Toronto. How would North American audiences react to such English eccentricities? Tony Stratton Smith had employed an old friend and contact Ed Goodgold (who had previously managed Sha Na Na) as their US manager, who would use his promoting skills (which often meant lying through his teeth) to find gigs for a virtually unknown English band even at smaller venues.

Certainly their music wasn't to everyone's taste – a lot of American blues rockers were no more prepared for a vocalist dressed as a woman or a flower or a bat or anything else except a man with long hair holding a microphone and screaming, but they persevered and, gradually, audiences started to understand what it was all about.

Suddenly, Genesis found themselves being compared to the likes of David Bowie and Alice Cooper in terms of Gabriel's stage persona, and musically to the UK's top prog-rock bands such as Yes, Emerson, Lake and Palmer, Jethro Tull and Pink Floyd – none of which, in reality, displayed any great similarity to Genesis whatsoever. With their battery of folky 12-string guitars, religious, mystical and mythical themes, and a wardrobe full of bizarre costumes, nobody sounded or looked anything like Genesis. "We were underway, we were heading somewhere different," said Tony Banks. "*Foxtrot* was where we started to become significant."

The band returned to England with their confidence levels continuing to blossom and grow, like a flower. A flower?

ABOVE: Happy days: Genesis, 1972

ABOVE: Peter Gabriel parks his bike, circa 1973

The transcendence of Angel Gabriel

On their return to the UK at the end of their first US tour there was another Genesis casualty in the form of Richard Macphail who had felt disappointed with the lack of support from their American label, Buddha Records, for *Foxtrot*. He was also concerned that the band were now moving into a more professional environment requiring a more professional crew - not helped by the technical problems he had partly been responsible for during their first brief visit to the USA a few months earlier. Macphail was making a good point because, in August of that year, Genesis became, for the first time, one of the headlining acts at the Reading Festival, billed above top performers such as Rory Gallagher, and Rod Stewart and the Faces. It was almost as if, from relative insignificance, they had snuck in through the back door and been promoted to top-half, premier league status.

What was needed to confirm their importance in the European music scene was a follow-up album to *Foxtrot*, and once again Tony Stratton Smith arranged for the band to write and rehearse at a large country house in Chessington, Surrey, before moving on once again to a room beneath the Una Billings School of Dance in Shepherd's Bush. Three months were allocated to come up with the new album but, having spent so much time travelling around America with very little opportunities to write or improvise together, it was soon clear that the band were short of material and pushed for time to achieve that deadline.

To fill the gap, Strat came up with the idea of releasing *Genesis Live,* put together from material scheduled for the American radio show 'King Biscuit Flower Hour' that had been recorded at UK shows in Leicester and Manchester. Remixed by John Burns at Island Studios, the band weren't too happy about its release as the sound quality was far from perfect (for that reason it was never actually broadcast in the USA) but Strat made the decision to put it out as a budget LP for sale in mass-market retail outlets. It worked, making it to No. 9 in the UK charts - their first Top 10 album. Peter Gabriel had insisted the album wouldn't be released in the USA but eventually it was, distributed by Buddha Records.

With more writing time now available, the lack of material allowed Steve Hackett to get more involved. The ironic result was that they ended up with too many long numbers for what would become *Selling England by the Pound* - their most successful album to date. Rising to No. 3 in the

UK charts, it gave Genesis their second Top 10 album in the space of three months and things had never looked rosier. The truth, however, in terms of the band's reliability and organisation, was a different story.

From October 1973 Genesis set off on a major tour initially across the UK supporting *Selling England by the Pound* before heading over to North America for six weeks. The issues had come to a head at a gig in Glasgow on 5 October when the band's crew (now minus Richard Macphail) had been unable to wire up the lighting rig safely, with the result that the show had to be cancelled, much to the chagrin of the promoter. Strat's virtual namesake, Tony Smith, had been involved with Charisma on the successful 'Six Bob Tour' back in 1971 and had considerable experience after working for several years for his father John's promotion company. Returning to their Glasgow hotel, Smith made it clear to the band that they needed to find some serious management or the mess they were in would only get worse. Little did he know that things were already worse. Much, much worse.

The band had never really had a proper manager up to this stage and it soon became clear that there had also been a complete lack of control over their financial expenditure plus inconsistencies in light designer Adrian Selby's book-keeping; the band had run up debts of over £150,000, which was why, despite their sell-out gigs and chart success, the band members were still on a wage of only around £35 a week.

It didn't help when the single from *Selling England by the Pound,* 'I Know What I Like (In Your Wardrobe)' became the band's first Top 30 hit, climbing up to No. 21 and scheduled for a slot on the BBC's *Top of the Pops*, but the band refused to mime to the song at the BBC studio. It was the final straw for Tony Stratton Smith in terms of his fairly loose control over the band and the split-loyalties he had sometimes had to deal with in supporting what was best for his own record company, Charisma. He informed Genesis that he no longer wanted to be in charge of their overall management and, when Tony Smith agreed to help the band sort out their problems, was happy to hand over the reins.

From 7 November to 20 December 1973 Genesis toured Canada and the USA for the second time but with someone actually capable of being in charge. From January 1974 the band embarked on another tour across Europe, the UK, Canada and the USA to continue promoting *Selling England by the Pound,* before returning to the UK in early May and heading almost immediately into Headley Grange in Hampshire to write and rehearse their next album. Originally built in 1795 as a workhouse for the poor, Headley Grange had been used as a rehearsal and recording venue over the last few years for such rock gods as Led Zeppelin, Fleetwood Mac and the Pretty Things. Arriving somewhat shocked at what was little more than a rather creaky, rat-infested and purportedly haunted old mansion that would have been perfect for a *Scooby Doo* movie, the band spent three months working and living in primitive conditions before moving on to Glaspant Manor in Wales to record their first double album, *The Lamb Lies Down on Broadway*.

Using Island Record's Mobile Studio with John Burns at the controls, Peter Gabriel's concept for a double album hadn't exactly been embraced by the other members of the band at what was proving to be a particularly difficult time for all of them. All were struggling with various personal problems, particularly Peter Gabriel whose wife, Jill, was in hospital in London giving birth to their first child; during the delivery she had suffered an infection from an epidural needle that had seriously affected her and their baby daughter's health and, understandably, Peter was spending a lot of time by their side. Even under such traumatic circumstances, his band colleagues, as ever, demonstrated very little sympathy.

As if that weren't enough, the film director William Friedkin (*The Exorcist*) had been impressed by a short story written by Peter for the back cover of the *Genesis Live* album and invited him to work on some script ideas. When Peter told the band he needed some time off in addition to his regular trips to London to visit his sick family, he was presented with an ultimatum: either get on with writing the lyrics for the new album or you're out. For three days, Peter disappeared but was eventually persuaded by Tony Stratton Smith to return to complete the album. Realising the chaos he'd caused

within the band, William Friedkin cancelled his project, but, for Gabriel, the seeds had been sown for a not too distant departure. As Mike Rutherford commented in *The Living Years*: "For the first time we felt that someone wasn't pulling in the same direction as the rest of us... something fundamental had changed."

Released at the end of November 1974, *The Lamb Lies Down on Broadway* was not particularly well-received by fans, or the media or, indeed, by any of the band members apart from Gabriel, but made it to No. 10 in the UK and No. 41 in the States. They set out to the USA yet again to promote the new album, beginning in Chicago on the 20 November and finishing in the same city on 4 February 1975. It was a long haul tour, haunted by myriad technical problems with a multiscreen projector and lighting system featuring up to 1500 slides that continually went out of synch or stopped working altogether. The album was performed in its entirety over 90 minutes in front of a baffled audience, most of whom had not heard it before. The tour was an accident waiting to happen and it occurred after just six performances of *The Lamb* when Gabriel made an announcement.

Six shows in (so only another 32 US/Canadian and more than 60 European concerts to get through), Peter Gabriel told them he was leaving once the tour was completed, and refused to budge. Everything, he said, had lost its spark and become soulless and the band's future (and his own) was being planned too far ahead in too much detail, limiting his need to explore other avenues and devote more time to the things that mattered the most to him. He reassured them that he would be loyal to the band through to the end of the tour, but that was it.

Genesis' Angel Gabriel would spread his wings and fly away forever.

MAIN IMAGE:
Genesis performing using white gauze to hide their stage equipment, 1973

ABOVE: Peter Gabriel takes to the air on stage, 1973

ABOVE & TOP: Enjoying the Surrey countryside, 1974

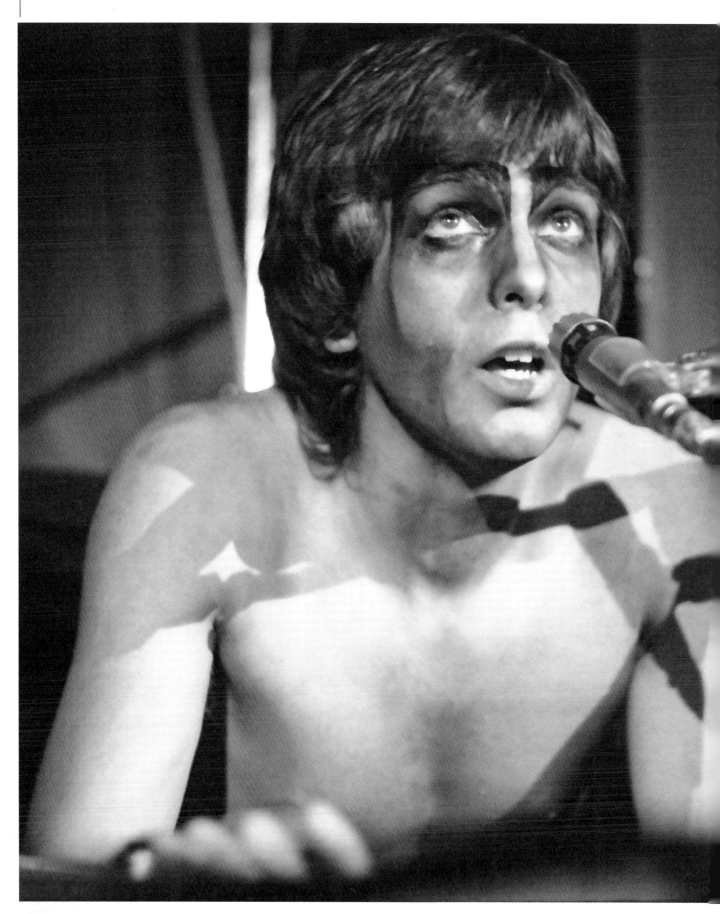

ABOVE: Peter Gabriel performing as Rael from *The Lamb Lies Down on Broadway* at the Empire Pool, London, April 1975

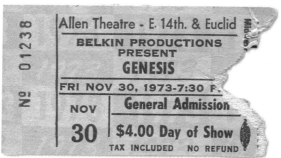

Allen Theatre - E. 14th. & Euclid

Nº 01238

BELKIN PRODUCTIONS
PRESENT

GENESIS

FRI NOV 30, 1973-7:30 P.

NOV
30

General Admission

$4.00 Day of Show

TAX INCLUDED   NO REFUND

TICKETRON
ADMIT ONE — SUBJECT TO THE CONDITIONS ON THE BACK HEREOF.

EVENT CODE	1206	NY. ACADEMY OF MUS
SEC LOC	12RORC	HOWARD STEIN PRES
	RIGHT	GENESIS
ROW-BOX	$7.50	
	D	8:00P FRI DEC 06
	NO/REF	14125392 271183
SEAT	1	PHONE 212 541 7290

CAPITAL THEATRE 326 MONROE ST

JOHN SCHER PRESENTS

GENESIS

PASSAIC NEW JERSEY

7:30PM FRI DEC 13 1974

26222612 1508/34

NO REFUNDS OR EXCHANGES

DATE/EVENT CODE 1213
RAINCHECK 7:30PM
ENTRANCE
L/C   B
OUTDOOR $6.00
EST. PRICE
08/15   TX 0.30
$6.30
TOTAL

20LORG   SEC LOC
L/C
III
B

III
SEAT ROW-BOX

EMPIRE POOL, WEMBLEY

JOHN SMITH ENTERTAINMENTS

presents

GENESIS IN CONCERT

TUESDAY, APRIL 15th, 1975

at 8 p.m.

SOUTH UPPER TIER

£2.00

TO BE RETAINED. See conditions on back

APRIL
15

ENTER AT
SOUTH DOOR
ENTRANCE

2

57
ROW
G
SEAT
70

C 14TH ST/3RD AVE

NTS   1207   40CBAL   SEC LOC
DATE/EVENT CODE
8:00P   LF CEN
ENTRANCE
40CBAL   K   109

1974 $6.50   K
2/6   EST. PRICE
$6.50   109
TOTAL

SEAT ROW-BOX

genesis

GAY & COMPANY y JF PROMOCIONES MUSICALES

presentan

GENESIS

VELODROMO DE SAN SEBASTIAN

GRADAS

Nº 1357

Nº 1357

PRECIO 275 PTAS.   domingo 18 mayo/noche 21 horas   PRECIO 275 PTAS.

entrada

Farewell to the acolyte

Making their way back to the UK once again at the beginning of February 1975, the band had just two weeks to prepare for a European tour that got underway in Oslo on the 19th and continued with over 60 shows across Denmark, Germany, Holland, France, Portugal, Spain, Italy, Switzerland, Belgium and the UK. Peter Gabriel's anti-climatic final gig was in Besançon, France, on 22 May 1975. It was meant to be the following night in Toulouse, but the show had been cancelled due to poor ticket sales. There'd be no more Genesis gigs for over 10 months.

The obvious questions they now had to consider were: should they continue as a four-piece instrumental band (as Phil Collins had suggested)? Or could they find a replacement vocalist and front man? And, most importantly, could any of them find the energy even to try? All needed to take some time off to consider their future. Phil Collins and Steve Hackett had already expressed frustration at the mess the band was in and both took more interest in other projects – Phil with his jazz-fusion band Brand X, which he had co-founded with the Welsh bass player Percy Jones, while Steve concentrated on his first solo album, *Voyage of the Acolyte.* Mike Rutherford spent some time working with Ant Phillips on his old friend's first solo LP, *The Geese and the Ghost* (although it did not appear for another two years). Tony Banks was also working on material for his planned first solo album.

After a period of recuperation and reconciliation, the remaining four band members made the decision to carry on, with the priority obviously being to find a replacement singer. A succession of vocalists – including some well-known faces such as Nick Lowe (ex-Brinsley Schwarz) and Mick Rogers (guitarist for Manfred Mann) – threw their hats into the ring,

but the more the procedure continued, and the more Phil Collins spent time prepping the hopeful auditionees as to how they should sing the songs, the more clear it became that they already had the right man. Although reluctant to make that giant leap from being drummer at the back to singer up front, the suggestion had already been made to Phil by various people that he should welcome the move; in reality, he had been backing up Peter Gabriel's vocals since *Nursery Cryme*, both live and in the studio, and the uncanny resemblance in their singing voices had often been mentioned. With pressure already being applied by Charisma for the next album, Collins reluctantly agreed, at least in the short term, to give it a go.

Despite all of the activity created by ads being placed for potential singers and the to-ing and fro-wing of hopefuls for auditions, the band made the decision to keep Peter Gabriel's departure a secret for as long as possible, although why that was considered a good idea (and how the truth wasn't revealed until August '75) is only known to them. Understandably they were nervous as to how Genesis would be received without Gabriel, but the news had to break at some point, so why hide it and make those concerns more obvious once the truth was revealed? It was the 16 August issue of *Melody Maker* that eventually leaked Gabriel's departure from Genesis with a front page splash, by which time the band had already set off to a rehearsal room in Acton, west London, where they were writing their first album as a four-piece, *A Trick of the Tail*

During the quiet couple of months after Peter Gabriel's final show, Tony Banks had focused on material for his first solo album until the decision was made that Genesis would continue as a band. From then on he concentrated on new, much-needed material for the band and also donated much of what he had already written towards what would become their most successful album so far. Co-produced by David Hentschel and recorded at London's Trident Studios, *A Trick of the Tail* equalled *Selling England by the Pound* by reaching No. 3 in the UK charts and climbed to No. 31 in the USA. It remained in the UK charts for 39 weeks and helped to write off a considerable amount of the enormous debts the band had accrued up to this point. Despite being pulled in two directions as to which way the band should progress in the future artistically (and financially), sighs of relief could be heard all around. *A Trick of the Tail* was well-received by all upon its release in February 1976 and is still considered by many to be one of Genesis' best ever albums – with or without Peter Gabriel.

The 'Trick of the Tail Tour' got underway in late March 1976 with over 35 shows across Canada and the USA and 25 shows throughout Europe. There was a new face and an old face taking part in the tour: Richard Macphail returned as their tour manager from April '76, while on the drum stool sat the brilliant Bill Bruford, previously the drummer for Yes and King Crimson, who had suggested to his friend Phil Collins that if he was handling lead vocals for the first time, why not bring him along to take care of the drums? It was the perfect solution to help Collins conquer his dreadful nerves over the first few shows, hands thrust into his pockets, hiding behind the microphone stand and referring to notes with shaking hands between songs. "It will be some time," he says later, "before I touch the microphone, remove it from the holder and actually walk around with it. Only when that happens do I feel it's official: I, Phil Collins, am a singer."

By the time Genesis' huge world tour came to its conclusion in July 1976, Collins had pretty much nailed it and taken on his new role admirably, to much acclaim. The band had been rejuvenated. Everything, it seemed, was going to be all right after all... Well, yes... (but, as in every chapter of the Genesis story) ...and no. Despite their survival and new level of success, not everything was tickettyboo. The problem, on this occasion, amid a sense of shuffling feet, came from the direction of Steve Hackett.

Genesis were back together by September at Relight Studios in Hilvarenbeek, Netherlands, to record their eighth studio album – the first to be recorded abroad, with producer David Hentschel once again in control. Despite *A Trick of the Tail* and *Wind & Wuthering* being released just 10 months apart within the same year, there was an expectation there'd be a shortage of material available, but Hackett was feeling that his capabilities as a songwriter weren't being taken seriously enough. He did have a point. Tony Banks had been credited on all eight of the tracks on *A Trick of the Tail*; Hackett had notched up only three, despite the feeling that the quality and importance of his guitar playing in creating the overall Genesis sound seemed to have gained more attention since Gabriel's departure.

For *Wind & Wuthering* Hackett had managed to net four songwriter credits while Banks had six; things had improved a little, but it was too little, too late. The success of Hackett's solo album, *Voyage of the Acolyte*, had demonstrated he was more than capable of writing a regular supply of quality material (his and Phil Collins's 'Blood on the Rooftops', for example, being considered one of the best tracks on the album) but it seemed to him that it was always down to who

ABOVE: Genesis with Bill Bruford (far left) in Central Park, New York City. April 1976

shouted the loudest. Always (and always had been), it was Tony Banks. To be fair, Banks had written some excellent numbers for the latest album, including 'Afterglow' and 'One for the Vine' but punk and new wave were just around the corner and the media were already distancing themselves from this group of public and grammar school boys who wrote songs about "cosmic sci-fi fantasy rock", as *New Musical Express* described it.

In the end, they actually had too many songs to squeeze onto *Wind & Wuthering* so three tracks were released in May 1977 as the first Genesis EP, *Spot the Pigeon*, the title linking the two Side 1 titles – 'Match of the Day' (celebrating the rituals of traditional Saturday afternoon English football) and 'Pigeons' (a pleasant enough parody of George Formby, played on a ukulele). Neither were standout tracks, to say the least, but Side 2, 'Inside and Out' was a much better effort clocking in at over six-and-a-half minutes with a two-and-a-half minute instrumental finale in Genesis' typical, multi-layered style. It could well have been selected for *Wind & Wuthering*; Steve Hackett felt that it was a strong number and, as the only track on the EP on which he was credited as co-songwriter with

Banks, Rutherford and Collins, that it should have made it onto the album. It was all further evidence to be added to his long-term exit-strategy plan in preparation for departure. He'd simply had enough.

From New Year's Day 1977 right through to 3 July, Hackett remained loyal to the band as they toured the UK, USA, Canada and Europe. For the first time they also took part in a short tour of Brazil, playing 12 shows at three venues in Porto Alegre, Rio De Janeiro and Sau Paulo to huge audiences of up to 20,000 rock-starved fans, gaining an enthusiastic response from everyone there including the local media. Some of the shows in Paris were also recorded and mixed for the band's second live album, *Seconds Out*. Released in October 1977 and featuring on record for the first time their new touring drummer, Chester Thompson (and Bill Bruford on 'The Cinema Show' only), the album represented some of the band's very best performances during their last two world tours and was well-received by media and fans – reaching No. 4 in the UK and No. 47 in the USA.

It was while the live album was being mixed by David Hentschel at Trident Studios during August 1977 that Hackett told the band he was leaving. Phil Collins was on his way to the studio to help with the mixes when he spotted Hackett near Holland Park Avenue and offered him a lift; Hackett waved hello but turned down the offer and said he's see him later. Strange, thought Collins, but when he arrived at the studio he was informed by Banks and Rutherford that Steve had quit. So much had he enjoyed recording his first solo album, *Voyage of the Acolyte,* that, he'd decided he wanted to pursue a solo career: "I'd got what I felt were all these very strong ideas that I wasn't able to get on *Wind & Wuthering*," he said later. "I had to take the risk to find out how good I was on my own."

Steve also explained why he'd refused to get into Collins's car that day: because Phil was the only person who might have been able to persuade him not to leave. Sliding doors. If it had been raining, or windy, or wuthering, maybe things would have worked out differently.

But not to be, Genesis were now down to three.

ABOVE: Mike Rutherford, April 1976

GENESIS
SECONDS OUT

THEIR NEW LIVE ALBUM
ON ATLANTIC RECORDS & TAPES.

GENESIS
In Concert, Plus Support
THURSDAY, 23rd JUNE, 1977
at 7.30 p.m.
(Doors Open 6 p.m.)
Arena £4.00
Harvey Goldsmith by arrangement
with Tony Smith presents

EARLS COURT, LONDON
(Opposite Warwick Road Exit, Earls Court Tube Station)

For Conditions of Sale see over

H 00007
To be retained

BLOCK
DD

Harvey Goldsmith by arrangement
with Tony Smith presents

GENESIS
IN CONCERT

THE APOLLO
Renfield Street, Glasgow

ON FRIDAY, 9th JULY, 1976
at 6 p.m.

STALLS

RR N° ----33

TICKET £1.75 inc. VAT
TO BE RETAINED
This Ticket is not transferable

MAMA CONCERTS presents:

GENESIS
In concert

Olympiahalle
München
Olympiapark

Sonntag, 26. 6. 77
Begin: 21.00 Uhr
Einlaß: 20.00 Uhr

DM 22.00

Arena
unbestuhlt

2639

Harvey Goldsmith and Tony Smith
presents

GENESIS
In concert
SATURDAY 10th JULY 1976
at 7.30 pm Doors open 6.45 pm
Tickets £2.50 inc. VAT
New Bingley Hall, Stafford
No re-admission
for conditions see reverse
to be retained and produced
on demand.
N° 09143
Scot. Auto. Edin.

172 WZB25
22 MNFLR
7 B6
gate/aisle
B6 ADULT
sec admission
CAS SJB01
B $5.50
row price
A $0.00
tax
7 02/77
seat

WINTERLAND ARENA
POST & STEINER - S.F.
###############
FRI. MAR 25 1977 8:00 PM
BILL GRAHAM/KQAN 95 ANN. C
G E N E S I S

MNFLR B6
gate/aisle
B6 R
sec/box row

ADULT
admission
7 $5.50
seat tax included

WATCH TOWER
GATE

B 11

LOGE $7.50

14C C 3
LOGE ROW SEAT

GENESIS
8:00 P.M.
WED. EVE.
FEB. 23
1977

GENESIS
IN CONCERT
VORVERKAUFSSTELLEN:
Sonntag
26. Juni 20.00 Uhr
München
Olympiahalle

NEW ALBUM

AVAILABLE ON CHARISMA RECORDS

MANUFACTURED & DISTRIBUTED BY PHONOGRAM LTD. PHONODISC LTD. CHADWELL HEATH ESSEX

Carry on, chaps

Once again, with Steve Hackett's departure, a lot of questions had to be answered. Would they, could they, carry on as a three-piece band without a lead guitarist? The answers didn't take long. By the time the live album *Seconds Out* was released in October 1977, the new three-man band had already written and recorded their ninth studio album *...And Then There Were Three...*

Mike Rutherford was a rhythm guitarist and excellent bass player, not a lead guitarist, but was willing to have a go – a lot easier than having to plough through the long and slow process of finding another competent player who would fit comfortably into the rather complicated world of Genesis. They'd been through that so many times before and just couldn't face it again. In some ways, Hackett's departure made things run more simply and smoothly for everyone: "fewer personalities to cope with, fewer arguments" as Tony Banks put it.

Instead, it was decided that the three remaining band members would continue to work as a trio on studio material, while two American musicians – Chester Thompson (previously with Frank Zappa and Weather Report) on drums, and a superb session guitarist called Daryl Stuermer – would take care of the live performances. The only problem was for two American musicians from Baltimore and Milwaukee to understand what the hell three boys from the English home counties were talking about. As Chester put it: "It would be the strangest feeling to sit in a room when you're supposed to be speaking the same language and not understand anything of what was going on."

With just the three of them in the studio, the band's songwriting routine seemed "almost effortless" and "liberating" according to Mike Rutherford. It had been agreed that the songs should be shorter and less proggy in response to the new wave scene that had arrived in the UK a few months earlier, meaning they could squeeze more numbers

onto the album. Of the 11 tracks on *...And Then There Were Three...*, three were group-written during rehearsals, with four more from Banks, three from Rutherford, but only one from Phil Collins. Having moved into a new house with his wife and two children in a residential part of London's Ealing, he hadn't been able to play drums at home in his normal approach to coming up with new ideas, so was playing and writing only while in rehearsals.

Ironically, there was one track on the album – 'Follow You Follow Me' – that had been group-written but was intended as a longer number. Atlantic Records had taken over from Buddha Records' half-hearted role as distributer of Genesis albums in the USA from 1973 with *Selling England by the Pound*. It was Atlantic's President, Ahmet Ertegun, who had recognised 'Follow You Follow Me' as a potential hit single and asked for it to be edited for the album. Although not too happy, the single was released in February 1979 and rose to No. 7 in the UK charts and No. 23 in the USA, making it by far their most successful single to date, and winning a new echelon of Genesis fans. Although *...And Then There Were Three...* overall hadn't been particularly well-received by the media, and certainly not by original diehard Genesis fans who found the new material just too poppy, it climbed to No. 3 in the UK charts and No. 14 in America. It was hard to argue that their switch to easier, middle-of-the-road material was a mistake. As Tony Banks put it: "Suddenly we were on radio and people couldn't ignore us." They also made their first appearance on the BBC's *Top of the Pops*, keeping everyone including Tony Stratton Smith, very happy.

All three of the remaining Genesis members were now happily married – Tony Banks had married his wife, Margaret, in 1972; Mike Rutherford had walked down the aisle with Angie in 1976; while Phil Collins had married his Canadian-born girlfriend, Andrea, in 1975 having been school sweethearts back in the early Sixties when they first met at their stage school in London at just 13 years of age. Andrea had retuned to Vancouver with her mother in the late Sixties following the death of her English father and she and Phil had rekindled their relationship when Genesis toured Canada in 1974. It was the sort of romantic story rom coms are based on but, in the harsh reality of life, Andrea had struggled to cope by herself with two young children while Phil, constantly on world tours, was very rarely at home.

Tony Smith had proved that not only was he now Genesis' manager but also a live performance specialist, and it was clear Genesis were becoming better known for their live tours rather than their record releases. 'The 'Wind & Wuthering Tour' had taken Phil Collins away from home for six months from January to July in 1977; the 'And Then There Were Three Tour' would be from March 1978, through to December, taking in all of the usual US and European locations. There was also an extra week for their first visit to Japan and a headlining slot at Knebworth Festival in June '78, in front of 120,000 fans. Apart from a three-week break in August, Phil would hardly be at their new home in Shalford, Surrey, for over eight months. Andrea had laid down some rigid conditions for their future together: if he went on the tour, she warned him, they wouldn't still be together this time next year. Collins, of course, went, because he had little choice, and when he returned from Japan in December, he discovered that Andrea was taking their two children back to Vancouver and, as far as she was concerned, they were through.

Devastated, but determined to at least try to rescue his marriage, Phil told his bandmates that he intended to move over to Vancouver to focus on his family. For once, Banks and Rutherford demonstrated some sympathy towards Collins and his personal need for time and space away from them; it was decided that 1979 would be a relatively quiet year, also providing them with the opportunity to concentrate on solo projects.

Tony Banks's first solo album, *A Curious Feeling*, released in October 1979 was loosely based on Daniel Keyes's 1966 novel, *Flowers for Algernon*, described by *Classic Rock* magazine as "lush pastoral English prog rock". It made it to No. 21 in the UK charts despite some very poor reviews. Mike Rutherford's *Smallcreep's Day* was also based on a book – Peter Currell Brown's surreal novel from 1965. After Bank's LP's disappointing reception, Charisma had the idea of putting Genesis stickers on the front of Rutherford's album, which made it up to No. 13. His reviews were generally no better, however – *New Musical Express*'s Paul Du Noyer describing it as "probably the biggest heap of pretension-riddled piffle I've had to plough through in ages". This was 1980, after all. Peter Gabriel's first three eponymous solo albums, on the other hand, had all made it to the Top 10 in the UK, with *Peter Gabriel 3* (as it's become known) making it to No. 1. Certainly he was doing ok all by himself (although Phil Collins did play drums on half the tracks) and it seemed unlikely that any other Genesis band members or ex-members would ever attain such an elevated level of success.

Welcome back from Vancouver, Mr. Collins. After the anguish of his failed attempt to save his marriage (he and Andrea were divorced in 1980), Collins had returned to the UK alone in April 1979 and was now living in his home in Shalford alone and unhappy. In an effort to keep himself busy he had worked on Peter Gabriel's third solo album, on folk singer John Martyn's LP *Grace & Danger*, and devoted some time to working once again with Brand X; he hadn't played on the band's third studio album, *Masques,* in 1978 but threw himself into their fourth, *Product*, in 1979. None of the Brand X albums had sold particularly well, but it gave him something to focus on, apart from drinking heavily. This was a skill he had honed while on tour with well-known imbiber John Martyn and with his new friend, Eric Clapton, who had also played on Martyn's album. Phil even allowed two of his Brand X bandmates to move into his home, which virtually became a nightclub.

In the end, Collins came to his senses; admitting to himself that such a drinking and drugging lifestyle was not his best option, he called last orders and kicked everyone out. With the help of a member of the Genesis crew, he set up a home-recording studio in one of the bedrooms in his spacious house and brought in a selection of drums, drum machines, a piano and keyboards. Once established he would spend hour after hour noodling around on the keyboards, writing sad ballads to reflect his rather miserable state of mind. For Collins, it was this noodling that proved to be a life-changing catalyst.

With the studio up and running and another new Genesis album scheduled for release in early 1980, Banks and Rutherford made the decision to keep Collins company by moving into his house to write and rehearse what would become *Duke*. It was agreed that all three band members would be allocated two solo tracks and Collins contributed 'Misunderstanding' and 'Please Don't Ask' – both good songs, but there remains some debate among the three of them as to whether or not Collins ever offered a little ditty he'd knocked out at home called 'In the Air Tonight'. Collins's recollection is that he did play it to the band but that Tony Banks wasn't too impressed by the simplicity of the keyboard parts; Banks, however, remembers it differently and claims he never heard it – if he had, he would have snapped it up for *Duke*. Rutherford isn't sure but feels that, as a three-chord song, it probably wouldn't have impressed him and Banks in its raw form.

ABOVE: And then there were three... Genesis, 1978

ABOVE: Genesis performing at the Omni Coliseum in Atlanta, Georgia, October 1978

ABOVE: Phil Collins on stage in character, October 1978

ABOVE: **Phil Collins, October 1978**

Either way, with or without it, *Duke* was released in March 1980 and recognised by fans as one of their best albums to date – or at least, since Peter Gabriel had departed; Tony Banks is an even bigger supporter and continues to maintain that this is the best album they ever made. Its reception from the media, particularly in the USA, was fairly positive, although the UK's new-wave-dominated press generally were far less impressed – "just a dry, empty daydream, a dreary doodle", said *New Musical Express*, while *Melody Maker* described it as a continuation of the band's already "homogenised sound". Did the band care? Probably not – *Duke* was their first UK No. 1 album and made it to No. 11 in the USA. On top of that, singles from the album achieved reasonable success as well; 'Misunderstanding' made it to No. 14 in the US charts (No. 42 in the UK), while 'Turn it on Again' reversed that success by climbing to No. 8 in the UK (No. 58 in the USA).

From 13 March to 30 June 1980 the band set off on what was a relatively easy 'Duke Tour' taking in six weeks in North America and, for the remaining eight weeks, concentrating on medium-sized venues spread across England, Wales and Scotland in response to the many UK Genesis fans who were of the opinion they had been left to simmer on the back-burner for the last few years. Around 100,000 tickets were available across the 40 UK shows and sold out within a few hours thanks to at least half a million applications being received. Genesis had become a huge draw across Europe and North America; world domination, it seemed, was only a matter of time. But Phil Collins had other ideas.

Collins had played some of his solo home recordings to manager Tony Smith, who had been very supportive and encouraged him to consider making a solo album. When Phil was asked to deliver a recording of *Duke* to Atlantic President Ahmet Ertegun's London apartment for his first listen to the album, he also took along some of his solo work, just in case he was interested. He was, and very impressed, so much so that Ertegun *insisted* Phil should make a solo album. The result was Collins working at the Townhouse Studios in Shepherd Bush, with Hugh Padgham, as co-producer through to January 1981, transferring his eight-track home recordings onto a 16-track machine and then bringing in a fine selection of musicians – Eric Clapton, bass players John Giblin and Alphonso Johnson, world-famous saxophonist and jazz club owner, Ronnie Scott, and even Earth, Wind and Fire's brass section, the Phenix Horns – to add overdubs.

Phil Collins's first solo album, *Face Value,* was released on 13 February 1981, largely to a positive media response. It went to No. 1 in the UK, No. 7 in the USA and Top 5 just about everywhere else in the world. A single from the album, 'In the Air Tonight', was released on 9 January 1981 and made it to No. 19 in the USA, No. 2 in the UK and Top 3 across the planet. All this from a homemade album he'd created by buying some keyboards and a drum machine before opening up his veins and letting a torrent of raw emotion gush out in gallons. Almost certainly it was kept off the top spot in the UK charts by the tragic murder in New York the previous month of John Lennon, whose re-released 'Imagine' followed by 'Woman' from his recent album, *Double Fantasy,* understandably dominated the charts for several weeks to come.

One thing was clear: Phil Collins, to paraphrase the great John Lennon himself, now appeared to be more popular than Genesis.

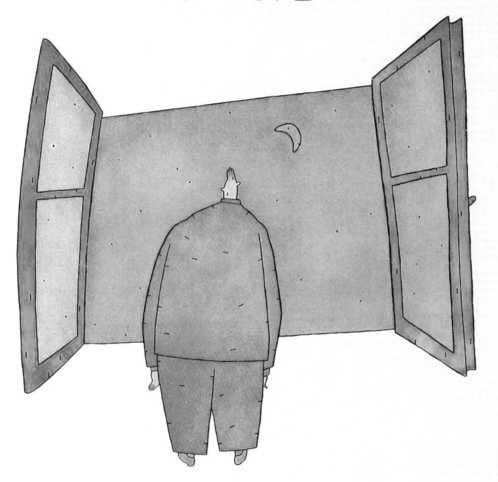

GENESIS

DUKE

NEW ALBUM AVAILABLE NOW
INCLUDES THE SINGLE 'TURN IT ON AGAIN'

AVAILABLE ON CHARISMA RECORDS AND TAPES

A home to call their own

When *Face Value* was released in February 1981 the band were already working on their next Genesis album, *Abacab* - their first LP self-produced and the first recorded at their own studio at Fisher Lane Farm in Chiddingfold, Surrey. An old Tudor building with a large, multi-vehicle garage that had originally been a cowshed, they converted the garage into a recording studio, which from then on was known as the Farm. While the studio was being constructed, *Abacab* was written and rehearsed in the farmhouse itself. The new location had a dramatic affect on the band's songwriting procedure and the atmosphere surrounding it; with so much more time available, and without having to worry about the costs if there were any problems or delays, everything seemed to flow almost seamlessly.

Banks and Rutherford had actually been rather relieved when Collins turned up at the Farm at all - so successful had he been by this stage that he could have just waved them goodbye and gone solo; already there were certain areas of the British media who were suggesting that was already the case and Genesis would not be around for much longer. In truth, such was Phil's love of Genesis and its music that it never occurred to him to leave - in fact he considered *Abacab* to be the moment when the 'new' Genesis was born. "*Abacab*," he said, "was the first time that we really talked to each other. That's why I was so excited by *Abacab* and that's why, as far as I'm concerned, the group almost starts there."

Another major change was the replacement of producer and engineer David Hentschel, who'd worked on the last four Genesis albums. In his place came engineer Hugh Padgham, chosen as a result of his contribution to *Face Value* and who, ironically, was renounced for the fast pace at which he worked. It was during Phil's session drumming on Gabriel's third album *Peter Gabriel (3)* recording the song 'The Intruder' that Padgham unintentionally created the infamous gated-reverb effect on Collins's drums, whereby, when recording, noise is cut off as soon as it stops, rather than fading away, making the snare drum sound noticeably sharper and

punchier and the drums more prominent in the mix. The recording technique went on to become the drum sound of the Eighties for bands such as the Police, XTC and Duran Duran. With no cymbals but an intensely loud snare, it was this sound that had made an enormous impact on Phil Collins's hit single 'In the Air Tonight', with a simple but effective drum break kicking in at 3.40 minutes. It's regarded as one of the greatest drum fills ever and became even more famous in 2007 when Cadbury used it in their memorable 'Gorilla Playing Drums' advert. It increased Cadbury's chocolate sales by around 7% and is certainly an image – and sound – that no one who experienced is likely to forget.

Once they'd heard Collins's *Face Value*, Banks and Rutherford immediately wanted Padgham to incorporate the gated-reverb effect on *Abacab*. It was also agreed that they should scale down the keyboard arrangements and the number of overdubs to ensure they didn't repeat themselves and end up sounding just like previous albums. Instead, they wanted something that would demonstrate a new Genesis more in keeping with the new wave sounds that had rolled through the music industry over the last four years. Tony Banks welcomed such changes and recalled later: "It was time to break with some of the Genesis traditions – get rid of the reprises, the extended solos, the big choruses… it meant you could write in a slightly different way."

In whatever way they chose to write, however, there were many diehard Genesis fans who weren't impressed by their more poppy, soft-rock approach and the lack of longer epics for which Genesis had become renowned. Some turned up their noses when the newer songs were played at concerts. As Phil Collins commented, "people who liked us in 1972 won't like us now", and he was certainly correct when they performed tracks from *Abacab* - the dreadful 'Who Dunnit?' and 'No Reply at All' (featuring Phil's best mates, Earth, Wind and Fire's Phenix Horns) - at a show in Holland and were loudly hissed and booed. This was not the Genesis that many long term loyal fans expected or wanted; some even suggested the band should change its name from Genesis to something else, because Genesis was a brand and they were letting down their fans by playing music that no longer represented that brand.

Abacab was written and recorded in 14 weeks at the Farm – actually slightly longer than previous LPs but it was clear from the band's overall demeanour that a great deal of stress and tension had been relieved by using their own studio facilities and with no-one else in the room apart from, in the latter stages, sound engineer Hugh Padgham. As Tony Banks commented: "I think our playing is very un-self-conscious with just the three of us. Anyone else would make us play a little differently. When the three of us play together it's almost like being on your own, you don't feel inhibited."

Such was the positive vibe in the Farm that they actually recorded enough material to fill a double album, although eventually decided against it. (Three of the tracks from the *Abacab* sessions were later released as their second EP *3x3* in May 1982.) Released in September 1981, whatever the opinions of some long-term fans, *Abacab* made it to No. 1 in the UK and No. 7 in the USA, although sales of singles from the album were slightly disappointing, with only the album's title track making it into the UK Top 10. A three-month 'Abacab Tour' got underway in late September concluding with three nights at Wembley Arena and four at the National Exhibition Centre in Birmingham just before Christmas.

The 'Abacab Tour' was also notable for being the first time the band made use of Vari-Lite – a computer-controlled intelligent lighting system that had been demonstrated to them at the Farm by Rusty Brutsche, co-founder of an American company called Showco, as a potential special effect for live performances. An innovation in stage lighting at the time, the system so impressed Tony Smith and the band that they took out shares in the company. At stadia of the sorts of enormous sizes they were now filling across the world, it had a dramatic impact on the live performances of a band no longer renowned for any on-stage activities apart from Phil Collins leaping about with a tambourine. As Tony Banks put it:

"The bigger the venue you're playing, the less important the guys on stage are. We used to sit dummies on the stage for the lighting rehearsals, which in my case was pretty much as mobile as me."

Vari-Light was another feather in the Genesis cap during a year that had been a huge success for all concerned and there seemed to be no reason why 1982 should be any different. It wasn't – things just seemed to get bigger and better, month by month. Following the successful *3x3* EP in May, which just crept into the UK Top 10 (while the main track 'Paperlate' reached No. 32 in the US charts), they followed it up with their third live album *Three Sides Live* the following month – another double LP that made it to No. 2 in the UK and No. 10 in the USA. With no studio album to support, the band set off on a two-month North American and European 'Three Side Live Tour' from 1 August through to 30 September 1982.

Such was the level of confidence flowing through the band member's veins at that stage that they even reunited with Peter Gabriel at the Milton Keynes Bowl on 2 October to take part in the 'Six of the Best' concert put together as a fund-raiser for the World of Music, Arts and Dance (WOMAD) Festival. WOMAD had managed to run up debts of almost £190,000 as the result of disappointing ticket sales for the first WOMAD Festival that year. Such was the seriousness of the situation that Peter had received threatening phone calls from people who were owed money.

Tony Smith spoke to the band to see what could be done and five of Peter's former bandmates were more than happy to come to his aid. In the end, Steve Hackett had to travel to the event from South America and arrived in time only for the encores. Anthony Phillips was initially approached to see if he'd be interested in taking part, which he was, but sadly it never happened. Chester Thompson and Daryl Stuermer also played their role on stage and, despite the band's lack of time to rehearse old material for more than one or two days at the Hammersmith Odeon, plus torrential rain that did its best to dampen the 47,000 audience's spirits, the show proved to be

ABOVE: **New stage line-up with Daryl Stuermer (second left) and Chester Thompson on drums. 1981**

a great success. In his usual style, and unknown to the other Genesis band members, Gabriel was carried out onto the stage in a coffin, perhaps an indication of his short-term future if things didn't go to plan. Thankfully they did, and the event raised sufficient funds for Peter to pay off his debts and keep WOMAD running as a uniquely inspiring annual event through to this day.

As 1983 approached it became another period of solo projects. Mike Rutherford's second solo album *Acting Very Strange* was released on 7 September 1982 but not well received, largely due to criticism of Rutherford's poor vocals on what were described as 'weak' songs.

Phil Collins's second offer, *Hello I Must be Going*, released on 5 Nov 1982, needless to say, was considerably more successful than Mike's effort. Much more soul and R&B-influenced than *Face Value*, the album received very mixed reviews but the public bought sufficient numbers to help it climb to No. 2 in the UK, No. 8 in the US and No.1 in Canada. Collins also found himself much in demand as a drummer and producer, working with the likes of Anni-Frid from Abba, whose solo album *Something's Going On* was a No. 1 album in Sweden and Top 20 in the UK; during 1982 he also drummed on Robert Plant's solo LP *Pictures at Eleven* – another Top 5 album in both the UK and US – and toured with Plant for the six-week North American stage of the tour to support his *The Principle of Moments* album in August/September 1983.

Tony Banks, on the other hand, kept himself busy by scoring

ABOVE: Genesis onstage at the Poplar Creek Music Theater, Illinois, October 1982

the soundtrack for Michael Winner's dreadful film *The Wicked Lady*, released in July 1983, and his own solo LP *The Fugitive* released at around the same time, which just made it into the UK Top 50.

This was also the time when Tony Stratton Smith, approaching the age of 50, decided it was time to concentrate more on the sorts of things he now found more interesting – a stable of race horses, for example – his lifelong passion – and he had also become involved in the film industry having raised funds from contacts in the music industry to finance Charisma's biggest stars, Monty Python, produce their first film, *Monty Python and the Holy Grail* in 1975. He went on to produce the

film *The Odd Job,* a comedy written by and starring Monty Python's Graham Chapman, and *Sir Henry at Rawlinson End*, written and narrated by another Charisma star, ex- Bonzo Dog Doo-Dah Band leader Vivian Stanshall.

Strat also worked as a screenwriter and producer on such movies as *Eye of the Dictator* – a documentary about the German Propaganda Ministry during WWII under the control of the Nazi, Dr Joseph Goebbels. Sadly, Strat never got to see the film released in 1988. Having sold Charisma to Richard Branson's Virgin Records in 1983 to enjoy his new interests, he died of cancer in London on 19 March 1987 at the age of 53. He was a great loss to everyone involved in Genesis, as he was

to other artists. As Peter Gabriel later said: "He was a wonderful man to have working behind us, really driven and with a great soul. He worked exceptionally hard for all his artists..." All were agreed there'd never be another Tony Stratton Smith. Steve Hackett was equally heartfelt in his praise: "Tony was very much a man of his passions and I miss him greatly. I wish I could press his hand warmly and tell him, 'You are the reason, more than any other person perhaps, that the band made it.'"

The first Charisma/Virgin LP release from Genesis, in October 1983, was the eponymous *Genesis,* the title chosen as a way to relaunch the band's new sound and style and reassure the world they were still alive and kicking, despite the myriad rumours that Phil Collins was leaving and Genesis were no more. An all-group-written LP and the first to be recorded and mixed at the, now completed, brand new studio at the Farm in Chiddingfold, *Genesis* was certainly better-received than the previous album *Abacab* and almost equalled it in its chart performances of No. 1 in the UK and No. 9 in the USA, but it was still considered something of a disappointment to many fans, old and new. Four singles were released from the album, with 'Mama' going on to become their first Top 5 hit in the UK at No. 4, but only reaching No. 73 in the USA, despite the huge impact of Collins's gated-reverb drums so suited to US stadium rock. Track two, 'That's All' rated better in America, climbing to No. 6.

With the American 'Mama Tour' from November 1983 through to February 1984, the band concentrated on their popularity in the USA, with the tour finishing after five nights at the Birmingham NEC – the only venue in Europe. The last night on 29 February 1984 was a charity event in aid of the Prince of Wales Trust, attended by Prince Charles and Princess Diana, who was said to be a big fan of Phil Collins and became a fan of Genesis as well when he arranged for all of their albums to be delivered to her. It was all very worthy but not very rock 'n' roll and seen by some – especially UK music magazines – as posh, rich and famous ex-public school boys playing rather insipid music to even posher, richer and more famous ex-public school boys and girls. It was true, up to a point, but did it matter? In reality, it would be quite some time before the three members of Genesis (and the Prince and Princess of Wales) would cross paths once again.

GEN N7 A 11 ADMISSION ADULT
EVENT CODE $ 12.75 .25 PARKING INCL $ 12.75
CC .75 PRICE CONTEMPORARY PRESENTS AT
N7 SECTION LLOYD NOBLE CENTER
CA 29X SECTION AN EVENING WITH
A 11 G E N E S I S
ROW SEAT THURSDAY
OSA2021
A121483 JANUARY 19, 1984 8:00 PM

BIRMINGHAM INTERNATIONAL ARENA
NATIONAL EXHIBITION CENTRE
JO CHESTER FOR
TONY SMITH AND BLOCK
HIT & RUN MUSIC 17
PRESENT
*** G E N E S I S *** ROW
DOORS OPENING 6:00PM A
OFFICIAL MERCHANDISE
ON SALE INSIDE ARENA SEAT
27
£ 7.50 MONDAY WEST
20TH SEP STAND
1982
8:00PM
(Including VAT)
TO BE RETAINED (plans & conditions see reverse)

SEC. ROW SEAT
REAR STAGE
34 C 17
NORTH
Retain Stub – Good Only
No Exchange — No Refund
TUES. NOV.22
8:00 P.M. 1983
Davis Printing Limited
GENESIS
PRICE 13.64+RST 1.36 $15.00
ADMIT ONE. Entrance by Main Door or by Church Street Door.
Maple Leaf Gardens LIMITED

CO COGEN EVENING·STAR PRESENTS
EVENT IN CONCERT
GEN VALID FOR
COL ADUL
SEC ADMISSION GENESIS
CAS IP ATTACHED VETS MEMORIAL COLISEUM
5 $ 12.50 WED AUG 11.1982 8PM
ROW PRICE
P $ .5952 FLOOR SEC. COL P ADULT
TAX ADMISSION
9 08/11 E 5 9 $ 12.50
SEAT SEC ROW/BOX SEAT TAX INCLUDED

BIRMINGHAM INTERNATIONAL ARENA
NATIONAL EXHIBITION CENTRE
JO CHESTER AND TONY BLOCK
SMITH FOR HIT AND 04
RUN MUSIC PRESENT
GENESIS ROW
Q
COMMENCING 8:00PM
DOORS OPEN 6:00PM SEAT
93
£ 6.50 WEDNESDAY EAST
23RD DEC STAND
1981
8:00PM
(Including VAT)
TO BE RETAINED (plans & conditions see reverse)

F0113 SEC 5 N 8 ADULT
EVENT CODE SECTION/AISLE ROW/BOX SEAT ADMISSION
$ 13.50 LOGE EAST 13.50
PRICE
CC1.25 * * *
SEC 5 AVALON ATTRACTIONS
SECTION/AISLE
CA 29X BRINGS YOU
N 8 G E N E S I S
ROW/BOX SEAT
OPL1007 AT THE FABULOUS FORUM
A21NOV3 FRI JAN 13 1984 7:30 PM

F0112 SEC 8 16 4 ADULT
EVENT CODE SECTION/AISLE ROW/BOX SEAT ADMISSION
$ 13.50 COLONNADE EAST 13.50
PRICE
CC1.25 * * *
SEC 8 AVALON ATTRACTIONS
SECTION/AISLE
MIA 53X BRINGS YOU
16 4 G E N E S I S
ROW/BOX SEAT
CCP1039 AT THE FABULOUS FORUM
A14NOV3 THU JAN 12 1984 7:30 PM

Mike Scheller Concerts Presents:
Genesis
Concert '81
Montag, 5. Oktober '81 · 20.00 Uhr
Bremen – Stadthalle 1
VA.NR. 13 No 129

MADISON SQUARE GARDEN
Fri. Eve. NOV. 18 1983
HALL OF FAME LOUNGE BOX
PERF. 2
ARCUS-SIMPLEX-BROWN, INC. N.Y.C.

madison square garden
Pennsylvania Plaza. 7th Ave. 31st to 33rd Sts.
AN EVENING WITH
GENESIS
PERF. 2 HALL OF FAME LOUNGE BOX

GENESIS 8:00 P.M. FRI. EVE. NOV. 18 1983
HALL OF FAME LOUNGE BOX
BOX SEAT PERF. 2

The good, the bad, the ugly

Following the 'Mama Tour' coming to an end in February 1984, it would be almost two years before Genesis would get back together again to make music. In the meantime, there were several solo projects to get involved in, some much bigger than others.

Mike Rutherford's Mike and the Mechanics project got underway in 1984 but was never intended to be a band, just a group of musicians who would help Rutherford on a solo album while Collins worked on his third solo release, *No Jacket Required*. Rutherford had asked manager Tony Smith and their record company, Hot and Run, if they could come up with a list of possible musicians to help him write and record a new album; their response was a list of 10, with Chris Neil (as producer) and B.A. Robertson (as singer/songwriter) at the top of the list. They travelled to George Martin's studio in Montserrat (one of the Leeward Islands in the West Indies) for three weeks to write and record backing tracks before returning to the UK to lay down some vocals. Chris Neil knew Paul Young (Sad Café) very well, while B.A. Robertson knew Paul Carrack (previously with Ace and Squeeze) – two of the best vocalists in the UK – so they were invited down to the Farm to take part. The result, almost accidently, was the creation of Mike and the Mechanics. Their debut album *Mike + the Mechanics* was released in October 1985 and made it to the Top 30 in the USA, while the single 'All I Need is a Miracle' climbed to No. 5 in the Billboard Hot 100.

It was a positive welcome for Rutherford after such disappointing solo success with his two previous albums and won him some much-needed glory, certainly in comparison to the other Genesis members, Tony Banks, Peter Gabriel and Steve Hackett, none of whom had enjoyed any great solo achievements since the early 1980s. One thing was for sure – none of them could compare to Phil Collins as a solo performer. His career had rocketed into a higher echelon altogether.

He'd been working at Townhouse Studios in London

recording *No Jacket Required* when he received an unexpected phone call from Bob Geldof in November 1984, wondering if he might want to take part in the recording of a superstar single to raise money for famine relief in Ethiopia. Collins was happy to take part, playing drums on the Band Aid single 'Do They Know it's Christmas', which went to No. 1 in the UK and raised around £8 million for the cause – far more than had been expected. As a result, some of the biggest concerts the world has ever seen took place primarily in the UK and USA on 13 July 1985 and raised an awful lot more.

One of the most memorable episodes during the day, of course, was Phil Collins being the only performer to appear at London's Wembley Stadium and Philadelphia's JFK Stadium on the same day. After performing 'Against All Odds (Take a Look at Me Now')', 'In the Air Tonight' and five other numbers alongside Sting to 75,000 fans, including his new best friends the Prince and Princess of Wales, Collins was whisked off to Heathrow Airport and flown to Philadelphia on Concorde. There he would perform his same two solo songs as well as playing drums for his friend Eric Clapton, and with Led Zeppelin's Robert Plant, guitarist Jimmy Page and bass player John Paul Jones as part of what should have been the closest thing to a Led Zeppelin reunion ever seen since the death of drummer John Bonham in 1980. Unfortunately it proved to be a dreadful, buttock-clenching performance, for which Jimmy Page laid all of the blame onto Phil Collins's. It's true that Phil didn't know the material very well and hadn't rehearsed with them, and the stage monitors weren't functioning properly so he couldn't hear half of what was going on, but the band's overall performance (including second drummer, Chic's Tony Thompson) had been equally poor – so much so that the recording was virtually destroyed by Zeppelin's management in an effort to prevent anyone else ever seeing it; if you can find it online, it's clear that Led Zeppelin didn't know what they were doing either. It was a shame, but did it matter? Live Aid raised £150 million for famine relief. And Phil Collins, it appeared (apart from the Led Zeppelin incident), could now all but walk on water

It was an atmosphere that had been noted by his Genesis bandmates, all of who were a little miffed not to have been invited to take part in Live Aid. As Tony Banks put it: "It was one of those events that became Phil's thing and not ours. I didn't even see it on TV. I felt all the time that we should be there. I just didn't want to watch it." Perhaps he would have been prepared to switch on his TV if he'd known what a disaster Phil's involvement in the Led Zeppelin reunion would prove to be...

Collins's third LP *No Jacket Required* – regarded by many as his best solo work – was released in January '85 and made it to No. 1 just about everywhere in the world (except, for some strange reason, Austria, where it got stuck at No. 11). The 'No Jacket Required Tour' took him around the world from February until July 1985 and, following Live Aid, he was asked to take part in an episode of the hugely popular TV show *Miami Vice*, playing the character 'Phil the Shill' – a British TV presenter with close contacts to Miami drug dealers. Just over a year later Collins went on to take the leading role in the film *Buster*, a romantic/heist comedy loosely telling the story of Buster Edwards, one of the Great Train Robbers involved in the theft of over £2.5 million from a Royal Mail train in 1963. The film was released in 1988 to very mixed reviews, although Collins's performance alongside the actress Julie Walters was largely considered a success. Ironic, perhaps, that it was around this time Phil Collins found some time during his busy workaholic schedule to relax, for the first time ever, with a hobby – constructing an impressive model railway in his cellar. "Completely different from anything else I've done in my life," he said. "I build the models, I make the scenery, and I get satisfaction from it."

By late 1985 Genesis had not played or even spent time together for over 20 months when the decision was taken to return to the Farm in September to begin their 13th studio album, *Invisible Touch*, with High Padgham once again behind the recording desk – a brand new one that had only just been completed. For the first time ever their recording process at the Farm was also filmed by the BBC for a Genesis *Old Grey Whistle Test* Special broadcast in 1986.

Although receiving media criticism for being very Phil Collins-dominated upon its release in June 1986, *Invisible Touch* went on to become their best-selling album to date – and the first to be released as an LP, cassette and Compact Disc, becoming the best-selling CD since the new format's arrival in 1982. Five singles were taken from the album, all making it to Top 25 in the UK and more impressively Top 5 in the USA, including the title track 'Invisible Touch' becoming and remaining their only US No. 1. 'Land of Confusion' was the most successful UK single at No. 14, largely due to the supporting video and record cover featuring the band's puppet images from the very popular UK satirical sketch show *Spitting Image*.

As always, a new album meant a new tour, and the 'Invisible Touch Tour' set off, with Chester Thompson and Daryl Stuermer in tow, in September 1986, taking in 112 shows across 59 cities in 16 countries including the US, Europe, Japan and, for the first and only time, Australia and New Zealand. It was also the first time for a Genesis tour to be sponsored, by Michelob Beer, with the deal including a TV commercial featuring Genesis performing 'Tonight, Tonight, Tonight' – a concept not particularly welcomed by all in having a song about drug addiction sponsored by a company selling alcohol.

The 'Invisible Touch Tour' concluded in July 1987 with one night at Hampden Park in Glasgow, one night in Roundhay Park in Leeds, and four nights at Wembley Stadium in London to over 300,000 fans. As before, the final night was a fundraiser for the Prince's Trust, with the Prince and Princess of Wales in attendance. As Tony Banks later described it: "I thought at the time, and I still think now, that moment was the peak of our career."

ABOVE: Promo shoot for the 'I Can't Dance' video, January 1, 1992

Having played to over 3 million people over 10 months, it had certainly been a hugely successful period for Genesis, although the tour was saddened just two weeks in by the death of Mike Rutherford's father, William. In a way his father would no doubt have approved, Mike Rutherford carried on with six shows in Chicago before flying back to England for his funeral and returning to the USA within 24 hours for a show that night in Los Angeles. As Mike put it rather movingly: "I was showing my father how my life had been shaped by what he'd taught me – duty, honour, commitment."

Mike and B.A. Robertson (who had also recently lost his father) wrote 'The Living Years' just a few months later – a song about a son's regrets not to have addressed issues with his father before his death. Taken from Mike and the Mechanics' UK No. 2 hit album *Living Years* and released in December 1988, the single also made it to No. 2 in the UK and was a No. 1 in the US. Mike's autobiography, *The Living Years,* devotes a considerable amount of space to his memories and deep admiration for his father.

If the period from 1986-87 had been good years for Phil Collins, Mike Rutherford and Genesis, it had been an equally good period for Peter Gabriel, whose album *So* was released in May 1986 and made it to No. 1 in the UK and No. 2 in the US. Five singles were released from the album, all achieving reasonable success, particularly 'Sledgehammer', which reached No. 1 in the USA and No. 4 in the UK.

For Gabriel and Collins it was a classic example of two members of a world-famous band diverting in two totally different directions, but both achieving remarkable levels of success. Ironically, the band member who could be considered the most important in the history of Genesis is Tony Banks, whose solo career continued to trail almost invisibly in the wake created by his bandmates' impact on world music. His solo album *Soundtracks* was released in March 1986, featuring his music composed for two dreadful films – *Quicksilver* and *Lorca and the Outlaws* – neither of which, along with *Soundtracks,* made any impression on bestseller lists or anywhere else. It can't have been easy for him to continue plying his trade as a musician in the ever-darkening shadows left by those closest to him.

The invisible years would return for Genesis once again for another extended period of four years until various solo projects had all been put to bed. Phil Collin's fourth solo album *...But Seriously* was released in November 1989 and once again, made it to No. 1 just about everywhere in the world, including Austria, but not, on this occasion, Italy, where it only reached No. 62. Very strange. Six singles were released from *...But Seriously*, with four in the US and two in the UK achieving Top 10 status.

Mike and the Mechanics third studio album, *Word of Mouth,* was released in April 1991 and almost made it into the UK Top 10, eventually stalling at No. 11. Having been reviewed rather coolly by the press, it was a disappointment for all concerned, but not as obviously as Tony Bank's two latest solo efforts. The first, *Bankstatement*, inspired by the success of Mike and the Mechanics, was actually issued in August 1989 under the title as a band name. His third solo album, *Still,* followed in April 1991. Both were recorded at the Farm but neither made it into the album charts.

It was probably a relief for all to get back together at the Farm in March 1991 to begin working on the 14th Genesis studio album, *We Can't Dance,* with a new face behind the recording desk – Nick Davis, who had previously worked on Banks's and Rutherford's solo material. Released in November 1991, this was the first of their albums to be issued only as a CD, providing them with the extra space to produce what is virtually a double album, made up of 12 tracks including two 10-minute-plus numbers – 'Driving the Last Spike' and 'Fading Lights'. Needless to say, *We Can't Dance* received very mixed reviews but reached No. 1 in the UK and No. 4 in America, producing three Top 20 hit singles.

Record sales didn't ring any alarm bells as such, but 'We Can't Dance Tour' ticket sales certainly did ruffle a few feathers. With a six-month tour schedule due to commence in the USA at the beginning of May 1992 through to a closing show at Wolverhampton's Civic Hall on 17 November, it all looked very promising, but there were several problems along the way. At a show in Tampa, Florida, Phil was feeling so unwell with a terrible sore throat that he had to leave the stage after two numbers and the show was cancelled. In Europe, several shows had to be scaled down or cancelled altogether due to strike action carried out by French truck drivers, making transport across the Continent almost impossible. There were also some shows affected by disappointing ticket sales – something Genesis hadn't experienced since the early '70s. Peter Gabriel, on the other hand, seemed to be rising irrepressibly; his sixth solo album *Us*, released in September 1992, made it to No. 2 both in the UK and USA, supported by the 'Secret World Tour' the following year and leading to the release of his successful second live album *Secret World Live*, also released as a live concert DVD.

While there weren't any clear signals that the book of Genesis would be closing, perhaps permanently, very shortly, there were indications that the band's future was on thin ice. Behind the scenes, Daryl Stuermer was now a member of Phil Collins's touring band and had revealed one or two rumours to Banks and Rutherford that Phil was unlikely to return. Manager Tony Smith was one of only a handful of people who knew that Phil Collins's private life had once again entered the emotional twilight zone. He had married an American actress called Jill Tavelman in 1984 after meeting her at a nightclub in Los Angeles during the 1980 'Duke Tour'. Their daughter, Lily, was born in March 1989 and it seemed they were leading a very happy family life together, until Collins's path crossed once again with a woman called Lavinia Lang. She was another pupil at Barbara Speake's stage school whom he had dated during his time there as a teenager, as well as his first wife Andrea Bertorelli; Lavinia had gone on to join the well-known British dance troupe, Hot Gossip. It was Andrea who put Phil in touch with Lavinia, now living in Los Angeles, and they arranged to meet up when the 'We Can't Dance Tour' passed through L.A. in 1992. It led to a brief affair, which severely damaged his second marriage.

Collins's fifth solo album *Both Sides*, released in 1993, focused on the breakdown of his relationship with Jill; they eventually divorced in 1996. In 1994 he had added to their marital misery by having an affair with a 21-year-old Swiss woman called Orianne Cevey, who had been employed to collect Phil from Genova airport, deliver him to his hotel, then take

him on to a show that night in Lausanne and help him with any language problems. She must have translated something really interesting because Phil and Orianne would go on to get married in July 1999 and have two sons together.

With pressure both personal and professional building up to such a point that he felt he had to take action, in late 1993 he informed manager Tony Smith that he couldn't cope with his solo career and a role in Genesis anymore. He wanted to leave. Smith was sympathetic towards Phil's situation, but advised him to use this period of Genesis downtime to think about things carefully before making any decisions or announcements. Collins agreed. Just a month earlier, on 18 September 1993, he had happily joined up with Banks and Rutherford to perform at a fundraiser at Cowdray Ruins near Midhurst, West Sussex, to support the local King Edward VII Hospital, alongside Mike and the Mechanics, Eric Clapton, Queen and Pink Floyd. He must have known it would probably be his final live performance with Genesis...

By 1995 Collins had made up his mind; his career with Genesis was over. Tony Smith asked Mike Rutherford and Tony Banks to come over to his home in London for a band meeting, and Phil revealed what they probably already knew: he was leaving Genesis. Neither of them were particularly upset, and certainly not surprised. As Mike Rutherford put it: "The surprise was that he'd stayed with Genesis as long as he had, after all that had happened with his solo career."

On 28 March 1996, an official press release was issued by their manager to announce that Phil Collins was leaving Genesis. And that, surely, was that? One would have thought so. In reality, after some thought, Banks and Rutherford told Collins that they intended to replace him with a new singer and, in typical Charterhouse fashion, would make a cup of tea and carry on once again.

MAIN IMAGE: Genesis, 1992

MICHELOB PRESENTS

GENESIS

SUMMER TOUR

FRIDAY, MAY 22 DODGER STADIUM/LOS ANGELES, CALIFORNIA • SUNDAY, MAY 24 THREE RIVERS STADIUM/PITTSBURGH, PENNSYLVANIA • TUESDAY, MAY 26 RFK STADIUM/WASHINGTON, D.C.
THURSDAY, MAY 28 AND FRIDAY, MAY 29 VETERANS STADIUM/PHILADELPHIA, PENNSYLVANIA • SATURDAY, MAY 30 AND SUNDAY, MAY 31 GIANTS STADIUM/EAST RUTHERFORD, NEW JERSEY

© 1987 ANHEUSER-BUSCH, INC. BREWERS OF MICHELOB® BEER ITEM NO. 328-01 < >

WE CAN'T DANCE

genesis

ALVALADE,
22 JULHO
1992

№ 5227

ALVALADE
22 JULHO

№ 5227

BANCADA SUL
E RELVADO

4500 esc.

IVA ENCLUIDO A TAXA REDUZIDA

VOLKSWAGEN
presents:

genesis

TOURNÉE

BANCO ESPIRITO SANTO
E COMERCIAL DE LISBOA

ENTRADA

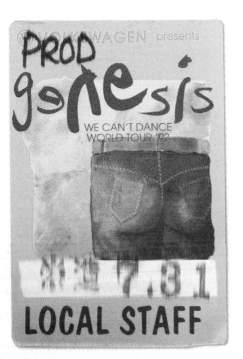

VOLKSWAGEN presents

PROD
genesis

WE CAN'T DANCE
WORLD TOUR '92

7.8.1

LOCAL STAFF

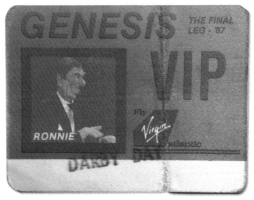

GENESIS

THE FINAL
LEG - '87

VIP

Fly
Virgin
atlantic

RONNIE

DARBY DAY

MANCHESTER NYNEX ARENA · WEDNESDAY 28th JANUARY 1998

SHOWTIME 8.00PM

Block:A   Row:C   Seat: 12 £20.00

Sub in association with Tony Smith for Hit & Run® presents

GENESIS
...CALLING ALL STATIONS...
...CALLING ALL STATIONS...
...CALLING ALL STATIONS...

Good News
von Blick

Invisible Touch Tour

GENESIS

Special Guest: PAUL YOUNG

Samstag, 13. Juni 1987, 19.00 Uhr
Kassa- und Türöffnung: 17.00 Uhr

Fussballstadion St.Jakob
Basel

Freikarte

Rückerstattungsanspruch auf den Kaufpreis

GENESIS

Samstag, 13. Juni 1987, 19.00 Uhr
FUSSBALLSTADION ST. JAKOB BASEL

№ 8108

EL EXCMO. AYUNTAMIENTO

PRESENTAN

Fly
Virgin
atlantic

OAKLAND COLISEUM STADIUM

BILL GRAHAM PRESENTS
AN EVENING WITH
GENESIS
RAIN OR SHINE
SAT JUN 20 1992 8:00PM

8MAY92 0WB372 ADULT

SEC 213   ROW 8   SEAT 22   PRICE 28.50

ADRID, Y MERLIN PRODUCCIONES DE ACUERDO CON HIT AND RUN MUSIC AND THE STATION AGENCY

E INVISIBLE TOUCH TOUR 1987

GENESIS
EN CONCIERTO

ARTISTA INVITADO **PAUL YOUNG**

ALAGA 10 de MAYO CAMPO DE FUTBOL DE LA ROSALEDA

ADRID 13 de MAYO (SAN ISIDRO '87) CAMPO DE FUTBOL V. CALDERON 22 h.

VENTA ANTICIPADA EN LOS CENTROS DE

The Last Domino?

So here we are at March 1996. We've covered about 30 years of the history of Genesis. Just 25 years more to go, all of which needs to be squeezed into a final chapter. Sounds impossible, but the truth is that not a huge amount has happened in the twists and turns of the Genesis story since 1996 apart, of course, from what is probably their final album, *Calling All Stations*. It would be nice to be able to report that the last Genesis album is in the same vein as the Beatles' *Abbey Road*, or even *Let it Be*, but sadly that's not the case.

When Banks and Rutherford returned to the Farm to start writing *Calling All Stations*, they found it difficult without Collins's vital input and started looking for a replacement vocalist straight away. Possibilities included Francis Dunnery (It Bites), Nick Van Eede (Cutting Crew) and David Longdon (Big Big Train), but in the end the role was offered to the Scottish singer Ray Wilson (Stiltskin), who joined, as a full band member, in June 1997. Wilson had, and still has, a great voice, and contributed to some of the lyrics on the album, but he is not really a songwriter and his input was minimal. Despite his best efforts, Ray did not provide the spark that Collins always contributed, perhaps more than had been appreciated. With him gone, of course, the band also needed a new drummer and brought in the combination of Israeli session musician Nir Zidkyahu and Spock's Beard's Nick D'Virgilio – both excellent players.

Calling All Stations was released in September 1997 and, despite everyone's concerns as to how it would sound, followed by some pretty terrible reviews in the media, the album made it to No. 2 in the UK, but only No. 54 in America, their lowest charting US album since *Selling England by the Pound* in 1973. A single from the album, 'Congo' just made it into the UK Top 30. A four-month European tour got underway in Budapest, Hungary, on 28 January through to Nurburgring, Germany, on 31 May 1998. Joining them on stage were Phil yahu on drums and Irish session guitarist and touring

member of the Corrs, Anthony Drennann. A North American tour planned to begin in November 1997, however, had to be cancelled due to very poor ticket sales. That must have been a blow to their hearts and heads – to recognise for the first time since the mid-'70s that in the USA there was no longer any major interest in Genesis.

The whole concept of replacing Phil Collins on lead vocals was always going to be tough for Ray Wilson; he gave it his best shot but the odds of success were always poor. Both Banks and Rutherford, ultimately, felt that they had not given Ray enough support and encouragement. Said Tony Banks: "Ray was always going to suffer comparison with Phil, and there was a high chance of failure... I thought Ray had a lot of talent. We could have used his talent better, because he showed so many moments of what he could do with us."

Ultimately, with disappointing album sales and very poor live ticket sales, there was never any chance that a second album with Ray Wilson on vocals would ever materialise; with sales even worse it could have seriously damaged Genesis' reputation. Wilson understood that, but was never happy about the decision or the 18 months he had to wait before he was given the official news: "They should never have tried it in the first place if they weren't prepared to see it through," he said, rather bitterly. "If they didn't have the balls to do it they shouldn't have done it at all." Manager Tony Smith agreed: "It was very sad after all those years to see Genesis sputtering and petering out. It was not the way to finish."

To take their minds off the reality of the future of Genesis, there would be a succession of solo material plus re-releases, Greatest Hits and boxsets over the 10-year period through to 2007. Mike Rutherford got in first with the Mike and the Mechanics fourth studio album, *Beggar on the Beach of Gold*, which made it into the UK Top 10 and included the hit single 'Over My Shoulder'. Five more Mike and the Mechanics

ALL FANS

albums would be released over the next 20 years between 1999 and 2019, with the last two – *Let Me Fly* (2017) and *Out of the Blue* (2019) making it to Top 10 status in the UK – a remarkable achievement for a little band created as a side-project by Mike Rutherford in 1985.

Collins wasn't far behind Rutherford in 1996 with his sixth solo effort *Dancing into the Light,* climbing to No. 4 in the UK. That same year, as a side-project, Collins put together the Phil Collins Big Band in tribute to one of his heroes, American drummer Buddy Rich. The Big Band toured Europe in 1996 with one of America's greatest ever record producers, composers and arrangers, Quincy Jones, conducting the wonderful Tony Bennett as guest vocalist; "I was," said Phil Collins, "in Heaven." The band released one album *A Hot Night in Paris* in 1999 but the project came to end that year when Collins began working on the soundtrack for the Disney animated film *Tarzan*, winning him an Oscar for the song 'You'll Be in My Heart'. Another far less successful Disney soundtrack *Brother Bear* followed in 2003. Collins's seventh and final solo album featuring new material was *Testify* in 2002; not well-received by the media, it became his first solo album not to make the UK Top 5. He did put things back to rights in 2010 with his very last album *Going Back*, made up of soul and Motown numbers that meant a great deal to him. The album made it only to No. 34 in the country where such brilliant songs had been composed but was a No. 1 hit in the UK.

From 1996 through to 2019 Steve Hackett continued to release a succession of studio and live albums via his own Camino Records and the German independent label, Inside Out Music. Although few of his records made much of an impact on the UK – and certainly not the US – album charts, there was some interest and praise among Genesis fans for his release *Genesis Revisited* in 1996 – made up of new versions of well-known numbers from his time with the band plus new or unfinished material. He went on to release *Genesis Revisited II* in 2012, featuring mainly once again Genesis numbers plus four tracks from three of his solo albums, and various guest vocalists handling some of the numbers; it went to No. 24 in the UK charts and sparked more interest in Hackett's remaining three solo albums – *Wolflight* (2015), *The Night Siren* (2017) and *At the Edge of Light* (2019) that all (just about) made it to the UK Top 30. A shorter version, *Genesis Revisited II: Selection* appeared in 2013, including Ray Wilson singing a new version of 'Carpet Crawlers'; there are also three *Genesis Revisited Live* albums since then; the second, *Genesis Revisited: Live at the Royal Albert Hall* also includes Ray Wilson performing 'Carpet Crawlers' live.

Banks had released nothing solo since *Still* in 1991 and it would not be until 1995 that another album would appear – *Strictly Inc.* – recorded with the band Wang Chung's vocalist and guitarist Jack Hughes and listed once again under a band name rather than a solo project; either way, it disappeared without trace. Since then, Tony has concentrated on his love of classical music with three albums released: *Seven: A Suite for Orchestra* (2004), *Six Pieces for Orchestra* (2012) and *Five* (2018). Banks certainly took great satisfaction from writing and recording this material and doesn't seem to be too concerned by regular overall analysis of his career – such as *Classic Rock* magazine in 2018 – as "the most overlooked solo artist from Genesis".

After the success of *Us* in 1992, Peter Gabriel's solo career also slowed down over the next 10-year period until *Up* was released in 2002, achieving reasonable sales to take it to No. 11 in the UK and No. 9 in America. It would be another eight years before *Scratch My Back* (an album of cover versions of 12 other artists) was released in 2010 followed by *New Blood* the following year. Both made it to the Top 30 in both the UK and USA. *And I'll Scratch Yours,* a companion album to *Scratch My Back,* was released in 2013 featuring a selection of Peter Gabriel songs performed by 12 other vocalists. Gabriel also had some success with soundtrack material during his later years, including *Birdy* (1985), *Passion* (music from *The Last Temptation of Christ* in 1989), *OVO* (music from London's *Millennium Dome Show* in 2000), and *Long Walk Home: Music from the Rabbit-Proof Fence* (2002).

Nor should we forget the hugely influential and inspirational band member as an important part the history of Genesis, Anthony Phillips. From *The Geese and the Ghost* in 1977 through to *String of Light* in 2019, Phillips has released no fewer than 33 primarily solo, instrumental, classical and baroque/ pre-baroque albums; none made it into the UK album charts but Phillips has been recognised as one of the most talented 12-string guitar players, and composers, of the last 50 years.

For the band, however, despite the lack of any new material, Banks, Collins, Gabriel, Hackett, Phillips, Rutherford, and early

drummer John Silver all got together in 1998 to celebrate the release of the four-disc box set, *Genesis Archive 1967-75*. The band followed this in 1999 with a new version of 'Carpet Crawlers' for the compilation album *Turn It On Again: The Hits*. In September 2000, Collins, Banks and Rutherford attended and performed at the Music Managers Forum in honour of the man who had been such an important element of their development and success, Tony Smith. And 2004 saw the release of the *Platinum Collection*, a career-spanning, 3-CD boxset. Basically, it seemed, as far as loyal Genesis fans were considered, that was that. Or so we thought.

After more than six years inactivity, in November 2006, Banks, Rutherford, and Collins announced their reunion for the 'Turn It On Again Tour', their first with Phil Collins back in the fold for over 14 years. Initially, two years earlier, the idea was to tour *The Lamb Lies Down on Broadway* with the classic

ABOVE: Mike Rutherford, Ray Wilson, Tony Banks, 1998

Genesis line-up of Peter Gabriel and Steve Hackett also on board. The five met in a Glasgow hotel to discuss the idea further, but Peter Gabriel never seemed to take it too seriously and the plan was dropped. Without Gabriel involved, Hackett seemed to lose interest as well, so the three remaining band members decided to continue with Chester Thompson and Daryl Stuermer returning as touring musicians.

Their get together was actually slightly sooner than anticipated when Banks, Rutherford and Collins performed an acoustic set at the tribute concert for Atlantic's Ahmet Ertegun at the Lincoln Centre in New York on 17 April 2007. (Ahmet had sadly passed away in December 2006 after tripping and banging his head at a Rolling Stones concert in New York in October that year.) Two months later the 'Turn it on Again Tour' got underway in Helsinki on 11 June 2007. The tour crisscrossed Europe for a month before ending spectacularly with a free concert on 14 July at Rome's ancient chariot racing-stadium, Circus Maximus, in front of around half a million people; the incredible performance was released on DVD the following year, entitled *When in Rome 2007*. A live album of various European recordings was released in 2007 as *Live over Europe 2007*.

On 7 July that year, Genesis also took part in the Live Earth concert broadcast to a global audience in an effort to help combat climate change and global warming, held at 12 locations around the world. At London's Wembley Stadium, Genesis took to the stage among other such luminaries as the Red Hot Chili Peppers, Madonna, the Foo Fighters, Metallica ...and Spinal Tap. Also in 2007, all of the band's studio albums from *Trespass* to *Calling All Stations* were digitally remastered by Nick Davis across three superb box sets: *Genesis 1970-1975*, *Genesis 1976-1982* and *Genesis 1983-1998*. In 2010

ABOVE: **Turn it On Again: Rutherford, Collins and Banks, 2007**

Genesis were inducted into the Rock & Roll Hall of Fame, which seemed a fitting conclusion for one of the world's biggest and most popular bands of all time. (Peter Gabriel was also inducted as a solo artist in 2014.)

From 2010 onwards there were various discussions and rumours about the possibility of a Genesis reunion, but Phil Collins had officially retired from the music business mainly due to family and health issues. Steve Hackett stated he considered the chances "possible, but highly improbable". Gabriel, similarly, thought there was only "a small chance" of a reunion. Banks and Rutherford remained non-committal. As the rumours continued, in 2014 Collins drew attention to the ridiculousness of even contemplating such an event: "Have people thought it through? It's not as if you're going to get Peter as the singer, me as the drummer. I can't play any more, so it's never going to happen." And would Gabriel be prepared to sing the songs Collins had recorded as lead vocalist since Peter's departure? Would Hackett be prepared to play songs such as 'I Can't Dance' or 'Mama'?

The nearest they got to a reunion in 2014 was when Gabriel, Banks, Rutherford, Collins and Hackett gathered for *Genesis: Together and Apart*, a BBC documentary covering the band's history, with a comprehensive 3-CD boxset as a companion release. As usual, long-term disagreements continued to smoulder when Hackett complained that he hadn't been given enough involvement in the programme and that his solo work had been largely ignored. The Ray Wilson period in the Genesis story was also not included. Hackett commented: "Look at the documentary and you'll get an idea of the priorities that come across." Bickering, it seems, still has its place in any project involving Genesis.

However, in 2015, despite his health problems, Collins surprisingly announced that he was coming out of retirement and now would be interested in a Genesis reunion! Loyal Genesis fans had their appetites whetted once again, but it was five more years before anything came to fruition. In January 2020, Collins, Banks and Rutherford were seen together in New York and, two months later it was announced on BBC Radio 2 that the three of them were getting back together for 'The Last Domino? Tour', taking in venues

across the UK and Ireland in 2020. Twice the dates had to be postponed and rearranged due to the arrival of the COVID-19 pandemic but got underway in September 2021 for 19 shows across the UK and Ireland. The three dates in Ireland were reluctantly cancelled due to Covid-19 issues, followed by the last four shows in Glasgow and London having to be postponed in October when one of the band members tested positive for Covid-19 and all had to go into self-isolation. The three remaining London O2 Arena dates were added to the European tour's 11 dates for 2022, while 22 new dates from November to December were confirmed for North America.

It was remarkable, all being considered, that the band were able to be touring once again from 2021 through to the following year. One can only assume that this really will be their last international commitment, playing to 15,000 to 25,000-sized venues across the UK and Europe, USA and Canada. Who would have thought they could be physically capable, or mentally prepared, even to want to embark on such a major international touring schedule during the crazy situation in which the world has found itself since March 2020? But then who can ever accurately predict what Genesis will get up to next? Performing live on an earth-orbiting venue having been flown there in Virgin Atlantic's Galactic? Who knows? Richard Branson was sort of their boss before he sold Virgin Records. With Genesis, anything is possible! And when Phil Collins was asked about the possibility of Genesis returning to the studio once more, to write and record new material, his reply was, "Never say never."

Let's face it: Phil Collins has never said never in his life. And probably never will. All being well, from September 2021, Genesis will perform once again, with Tony Banks, Mike Rutherford, Phil Collins, Daryl Stuermer and, for the first time, Phil's 20-year-old son, Nick, on drums, for the 'The Last Domino? Tour'. That sounds so young for someone to join a major European and North American tour alongside a group of seasoned professionals, but then you need to remind yourself how young the rest of them were when, in the beginning, Genesis was created out of a bunch of posh, talented schoolboys.

As to the end... God only known.

THE TOUR

TONY BANKS
PHIL COLLINS
MIKE RUTHERFORD

WITH DARYL STUERMER & CHESTER THOMPSON

FR., **29. JUNI 2007**
STUTTGART »SWR3
GOTTLIEB-DAIMLER-STADION

VORVERKAUF BEI WOM STUTTGART, KÖNIGSTR. 1 SOWIE ALLEN BEKANNTEN VORVERKAUFSSTELLEN.
MUSIC CIRCUS CONCERTBÜRO KARTENTELEFON: 0711-221105 · www.musiccircus.de

Tickets an allen Eventim-VVK-Stellen · Tickethotline: 018 05-570 000 (12 ct/min) · www.eventim.de
A PETER RIEGER presentation by arrangement with Tony Smith and Solo · www.genesis-music.com · www.prknet.de

TONY BANKS

Born: 27 March 1950

Place of birth: East Hoathly with Halland, East Sussex, England

Musical background: Tony's mother was a pianist who encouraged him to listen to classical and music theatre compositions from an early age; he particularly liked works from Holst and Ravel and, by the time he was a teenager, had progressed to composers such as Shostakovich, Mahler and Sibelius. He started learning piano at school at the age of eight and later taught himself to play guitar when influenced by the likes of Dion and Frankie Laine, and later the Beatles, the Beach Boys, the Kinks, Procol Harum, and soul music by James Brown and Stevie Wonder. At the age of 13 he moved to Charterhouse public school where he met Peter Gabriel and Chris Stewart and formed a band called Garden Wall; subsequently merged with another school band, Anon, featuring Mike Rutherford and Anthony Phillips.

Played on: Has played on every Genesis album.

Left Genesis: Has never officially left the band.

Where is he now? Apart from the 2007 'Turn it On Again Tour' (and 'The Last Domino? Tour' planned for 2021-22), Tony has concentrated on orchestral and film soundtrack composition since Genesis' virtual demise in 1998. He continues to live in the Godalming area of Surrey.

PETER GABRIEL

Born: 13 February 1950

Place of birth: Chobham, Surrey, England

Musical background: His mother, Edith, was from a very musical family and it was noted that Peter had an excellent singing voice while at primary school in Woking, Surrey. He began piano lessons with his mother at a young age and also developed an interest in drumming, getting his first tom tom by the age of 10. His early love was for religious music and hymns until, at the age of 12, he heard the Beatles' debut LP; later he was particularly

influenced by American soul music. When arriving at Charterhouse public school in 1963, he soon became a drummer and singer in a trad jazz band, the Milords, followed by the Spoken Word, another group he established during school holidays. He later formed Garden Wall with Tony Banks and Chris Stewart before merging with Mike Rutherford and Anthony Phillips's Anon.

Played on: *From Genesis to Revelation, Trespass, Nursery Cryme, Foxtrot, Selling England By the Pound,* and *The Lamb Lies Down on Broadway.* Also performs on *Genesis Live.*

Left Genesis: Officially left the band in August 1975 to concentrate on his solo career.

Where is he now? His career continues to be a huge success, having released nine solo albums, four film soundtracks and had a major impact on world music, human rights and political issues, co-founding the WOMAD festival in 1982. He lives in Wiltshire, South West England, where he created and now runs the Real World Studios.

MIKE RUTHERFORD

Born: 2 October 1950

Place of birth: Chertsey, Surrey, England

Musical background: Mike was living near Chester in Cheshire when he was bought his first guitar at the age of eight after seeing Cliff Richard and the Shadows perform at the Manchester Apollo. Within a year he had formed his first band, the Chesters, with school friends. He moved to Charterhouse public school in 1964 and formed the band Anon with Anthony Phillips – later to merge with Garden Wall becoming Peter Gabriel, Tony Banks and Chris Stewart. Mike was highly influenced at that time by the Beatles, the Rolling Stones, the Who, the Kinks, the Small Faces and Motown music.

Played on: Has played on every Genesis album.

Left Genesis: Has never officially left the band.

Where is he now? Mike formed Mike and the Mechanics in 1985 and has continued to perform and record with them during Genesis intermissions. Their latest album *Out of the Blue* was released in 2019. Mike continues to live primarily in Surrey but also has a home in Cape Town, South Africa.

CHRIS STEWART

Born: 27 March 1951

Place of birth: Horsham, West Sussex, England

Musical background: Wasn't particularly interested in music until he arrived at Charterhouse and befriended Peter Gabriel who subsequently taught him how to play drums. He soon became obsessed with drumming and was particularly influenced by Keith Moon of the Who, as well as the Beatles and the Rolling Stones, but admits he was never really very good.

Played on: Singles 'Silent Sun' (which also appears on the *From Genesis to Revelation* album) and 'A Winter's Tale'.

Left Genesis: Was officially fired by the band in 1968, due to his poor drumming technique, at the recommendation of producer Jonathan King.

Where is he now? Is well known for his humorous autobiographical books about his life as a farmer in Spain: *Driving Over Lemons: An Optimist in Andalucia* and the sequels, *A Parrot In The Pepper Tree* and *The Almond Blossom Appreciation Society*. He continues to live in Spain and has written several other books over the last 20 years.

ANTHONY 'ANT' PHILLIPS

Born: 23 December 1951

Place of birth: Putney, southwest London, England

Musical background: Was interested in music from a very early age and formed his first band while still at an independent primary school in London, taking up guitar at the age of 11 and being strongly influenced by Hank Marvin of the Shadows and later Eric Clapton. At the age of 13 his parents bought him a Fender Stratocaster and, soon after joining Charterhouse, in April 1965, he formed a band called Anon with school friends Rivers Jobe, Richard Macphail, Mike Rutherford and Rob Tyrell. Is regarded as the most talented musician at that stage of Genesis' early development.

Played on: *From Genesis to Revelation* and *Trespass*.

Left Genesis: Officially left the band in July 1970 due to stage fright and various health issues.

Where is he now? Having been listening to composers such as Sibelius at around the time he left Genesis,

Ant decided he wanted to expand and develop his music career, studying piano, classical guitar and orchestration at the Guildhall School of Music and Drama in London. In 1974, he qualified as a music teacher. He has been a prolific writer of library music and for film and television. He subsequently released more than 30 solo albums and has also contributed to albums by Mike Rutherford, Steve Hackett and the English progressive rock band, Camel, initially formed in Guildford in 1971. Anthony continues to live and work in that part of England.

JONATHAN 'JOHN' SILVER

Born: 22 February 1949

Place of birth: Oxford, England

Musical background: John took up drums at an early age and was a founding member of his first band at St Edwards, an independent boarding school in Oxford, influenced by the likes of the Beatles, the Rolling Stones and Randy Newman but also a big jazz fan, particularly Stan Kenton.

Played on: *From Genesis to Revelation.*

Left Genesis: Left the band in August 1969 (under pressure from his parents) to study at the School of Hotel Administration at Cornell University in Ithaca, New York, USA.

Where is he now? John played for various bands at Cornell University and always dreamt that he might be invited back to rejoin Genesis, but the call never came. He subsequently returned to the UK and embarked on a successful career in TV production for Granada and Thames Television, covering news and current affairs, and developing professional video editing systems. Lives in London.

JOHN MAYHEW

Born: 27 March 1947

Place of birth: Ipswich, Suffolk, England

Musical background: John took up drums at the age of 16 and played covers in pubs and clubs for various groups in the Suffolk and London areas. In 1968 he joined a professional band from Scotland, called Milton's Fingers, who had relocated to Surrey and achieved reasonable success on the university circuit. After a year with the band, John returned to London and advertised himself around town as a drummer looking for work. Genesis needed a new drummer after Jonathan Silver's departure and it was Mike Rutherford who called Mayhew to invite him to an audition.

Played on: *Trespass.*

Left Genesis: Was officially fired by Genesis in 1970 after recording *Trespass* as it was felt, despite his capabilities as a solid drummer, that he lacked the creativity to progress to the next level of the band's increasingly complex music.

Where is he now? In 1982 John emigrated to New Zealand and eventually Australia where he worked as a scenic artist and carpenter. He returned to the UK in 2002, moving to Scotland where he worked as a furniture craftsman for several years at the Charles Rennie Macintosh workshop. Sadly, on 26 March 2009, aged 61, John died in Glasgow as the result of a heart condition.

PHIL COLLINS

Born: 30 January 1951

Place of birth: Chiswick, west London, England

Musical background: Took up drums at the age of five and also completed drama training from the age of 14 at the Barbara Speake Stage School in west London, which had been established with help from his mother, June, an established theatrical agent. He landed several leading roles in London's West End theatres including the Artful Dodger in two runs of Lionel Bart's musical, *Oliver!* Ultimately he chose music as a career, rather than the theatre, and was largely influenced by the Beatles' Ringo Starr as well as jazz drummer Buddy Rich and soul music from Motown and Stax Records. He formed his first band, the Real Thing, while a pupil at Chiswick County Grammar School. In 1969 he joined John Walker's (of the Walker Brothers) backing band with guitarist Ronnie Caryl, with whom he went on to form the band Flaming Youth; they recorded one album (*Ark 2*) before disbanding in 1970.

Played on: Has played on every Genesis album with the exceptions of *From Genesis to Revelation*, *Trespass* and *Calling All Stations*.

Left Genesis: Officially left the band in March 1996 to concentrate on his solo career but reconvened with Genesis in 2007 for the 'Turn it On Again Tour'.

Where is he now? A vertebrae injury in his neck in 2009 has left him no longer able to play the drums but Phil has rejoined Genesis on vocals once again for 'The Last Domino? Tour' in 2021. Currently lives in Féchy, near Lausanne, Switzerland.

RONNIE CARYL

Born: 10 February 1953

Place of birth: Liverpool, England

Musical background: Also attended the Barbara Speake Stage School in west London and began his musical career in 1969 as bassist for Flaming Youth, featuring his best friend Phil Collins on drums. Auditioned with Genesis twice but was never officially a member of the band, despite playing in at least one gig with them in Aylesbury and possibly one or two others.

Played on: Didn't play on any Genesis recordings.

Left Genesis: Was never offered the position as his guitar style was considered too bluesy.

Where is he now? Went on to play in various outfits before joining the jazz rock band, Zox & the Radar Boys in 1973, which included Phil Collins and Peter Banks (ex-Yes and Flash). In 1996 Ronnie became the rhythm guitarist and backing vocalist for Phil Collins's group. He's performed with various other notable musicians including Eric Clapton, Tina Turner, Lulu, Maggie Bell and Gary Brooker, as well as releasing two solo albums. He currently lives in the Bordeaux region of southwest France.

MICK BARNARD

Born: March 1948

Place of birth: Princes Risborough, Buckinghamshire, England

Musical background: Played guitar for a band called the Farm and was recommended to Genesis by Dave Stopps who was running the local blues club based at the Friars in Aylesbury.

Played on: Didn't play on any Genesis studio recordings but performed on at least 30 gigs and on one BBC TV show *Disco 2* recorded in November 1970; the footage has since been lost. He also contributed to the writing and development of 'The Musical Box', the longest song on *Nursery Cryme*, before Steve Hackett took his place.

Left Genesis: Was officially fired by the band in January 1971 as his guitar style wasn't considered assertive enough.

Where is he now? Played for various other bands before establishing a career in audio engineering and founding Bel Digital Audio in 1975, based in Milton Keynes, Buckinghamshire.

STEVE HACKETT

Born: 12 February 1950

Place of birth: Pimlico, south London, England

Musical background: Attended Sloane Grammar School in Chelsea, London, and took up guitar at the age of 12 having previously learned to play the harmonica and recorder with a deep love of opera music and Johann Sebastian Bach. On guitar he was particularly influenced by blues players such as Peter Green and Danny Kirwan from Fleetwood Mac, Eric Clapton, Jimmy Page and Jimi Hendrix, as well as the Beatles and King Crimson. Was a member of four various prog-rock bands before joining Genesis in 1971: Canterbury Glass; Heel Pier; Sarabande; and Quiet World with his younger brother, John, a multi-instrumentalist.

Played on: *Nursery Cryme, Foxtrot, Selling England By the Pound, The Lamb Lies Down on Broadway, A Trick of the Tail* and *Wind & Wuthering.* Also performs on the three live albums, *Genesis Live, Seconds Out* and *Three Sides Live.*

Left Genesis: Officially left the band in 1977 to concentrate on his solo career.

Where is he now? Since leaving Genesis, Steve has released no fewer than 18 rock albums, six classical, one blues and 19 live albums, primarily on his own label Camino Records. Since 2011 his albums have all been released by the German pro-rock label Inside Out Music. Steve works and lives in Twickenham, southwest London.

BILL BRUFORD

Born: 17 May 1949

Place of birth: Sevenoaks, Kent, England

Musical background: Attended the independent Tonbridge School in Kent from the age of 13 and took up drums having been influenced by American jazz drummers on the BBC's *Jazz 625*. Co-founded a band at school called the Breed and also toured Italy for six weeks with a band called the Noise. Moved to London in 1968 and placed an advert in *Melody Maker,* which was spotted by Jon Anderson from a band called Mable Greer's Toyshop, which evolved into Yes.

Played on: Didn't play on any Genesis studio recordings but does features on *Seconds Out* and *Three Sides Live*, as well as three tracks on Steve Hackett's solo album *Genesis Revisited*.

Left Genesis: Was only ever considered a temporary stand-in drummer for Phil Collins when he took over on vocals. Bill officially left the band in July 1976 when the 'A Trick of the Tail Tour' across North America and Europe came to an end.

Where is he now? He formed his own band Bruford in 1977 and went on to play with various other bands before returning for periods with King Crimson and Yes. Formed his jazz band Earthworks in 1986, which was active until 2008 when Bill decided to retire as a professional musician. His book *Bill Bruford: The Autobiography* was published in 2009 and, from 2012, he studied for four years for a PhD in music at the University of Surrey. Also runs two record labels: Winterfold (rock-oriented music), and Summerfold (focussing on jazz). He lives in the Surrey Hills, near Leatherhead, Surrey.

CHESTER THOMPSON

Born: 11 December 1948

Place of birth: Baltimore, Maryland, USA

Musical background: Chester had an older brother who played drums but he took up the flute at elementary school before taking up drums at the age of 11. Highly influenced by jazz performers, particularly drummers including Tony Williams, Max Roach and Elvin Jones. From 1971 he studied music at Baltimore Community College for two years before joining Frank Zappa and the Mothers of Invention in 1973; in 1975 he joined Weather Report after being invited to audition by their bass player Alphonso Johnson, who later recommended him to Genesis when Bill Bruford left

Played on: Didn't play on any Genesis studio recordings but has played on solo releases from Tony Banks and Steve Hackett as well as one live Phil Collins album and the last five Genesis live albums.

Left Genesis: Left the band after the 1992 world tour as he wished to spend more time with his family. Expressed an interest in rejoining the band for the *Calling All Stations* album and tour in 1997 but on the condition he would become a full-time member, but this couldn't be agreed. He did, however, rejoin the band for the 'Turn It On Again' tour in 2007.

Where is he now? Chester moved to Nashville, Tennessee, in 1992 and worked as a session and touring drummer for a variety of artists. His role with Phil Collins, however, came to an end in 2010 over a disagreement concerning Chester's drumming on the 'Going Back Tour'. Formed the Chester Thompson Trio in 2011 and has recorded two albums.

DARYL STUERMER

Born: 27 November 1952

Place of birth: Milwaukee, Wisconsin, USA

Musical background: Elder brother Dwayne introduced him to music by Elvis Presley and Ray Charles and was later a huge fan of the Ventures. Took up guitar at age 11 and was playing jazz guitar by the age of 15. Formed his own jazz rock band, Sweetbottom, and was spotted by Frank Zappa's keyboard player, George Duke, who put his name forward to join jazz violinist Jean-Luc Ponty's band. He played on three of their albums before being recommended to Genesis as a suitable replacement for Steve Hackett.

Played on: Didn't play on any Genesis studio recordings but has played on all of Phil Collin's solo albums as well as solo releases from Tony Banks and Mike Rutherford and on the last four Genesis live albums.

Left Genesis: Officially left the band in 1992 but rejoined them for the 'Turn it On Again Tour' in 2007 and also took part in 'The Last Domino? Tour' across the UK, Ireland and North American during 2021/22.

Where is he now? Based in Milwaukee, Daryl has successfully continued his solo career as a musician and songwriter, producing nine solo albums as well as performing regularly with his own band.

RAY WILSON

Born: 8 September 1968

Place of birth: Dumfries, Scotland

Musical background: Comes from a musical family and his ambition from an early age was to become a professional singer, hugely influenced by David Bowie. Played in various school bands before joining Guaranteed Pure in the early Nineties, recording one album. Went on to join Stiltskin in 1994, a band put together by multi-instrumentalist Peter Lawlor to perform the single, 'Inside', specifically written for a Levi's TV ad, 'Creek', which got to No. 1 in the UK charts. It was included in the band's album, *The Mind's Eye*, which made it to No. 17.

Played on: *Calling All Stations*. Was also a guest singer on Steve Hackett's 2003 'Genesis Revised II Tour' and appeared on the album *Genesis Revisited II: Selection* singing 'Carpet Crawlers'.

Left Genesis: Has never officially left the band but the decision was made by Genesis in 1997 not to continue.

Where is he now? Released an album called *Millionairhead* in 1999 from a solo project, Cut_. Has since released six solo albums and formed a new version of Stiltskin in 2005, which released two albums. Ray currently lives in Poznan, Poland, and his latest solo album, *The Weight of Man* was released in 2021.

NIR ZIDKYAHU

Born: November 1967

Place of birth: Rishon LeZion, Tel Aviv, Israel

Musical background: Started playing drums at the age of 12 and turned professional at 16, inspired primarily by Gene Krupa. Nir has played drums for a number of notable musicians including John Mayer, Joss Stone, Alana Davis, Chris Cornell and Billy Squier. He is the brother of Tomer Zidkyahu, drummer for the rock band Blackfield.

Played on: *Calling All Stations* (eight tracks)

Left Genesis: Was only brought in for the *Calling All Stations* album and tour.

Where is he now? Currently based in Franklin, Tennessee, just south of Nashville, working as a successful studio session drummer.

NICK D'VIRGILLO

Born: 12 November 1968

Place of birth: Whittier, Los Angeles, California, USA

Musical background: Nick came from a musical family and is a multi-instrumentalist who started learning drums at the age of four. He is best known as the drummer for the American prog rock band Spock's Beard since 1992. He also toured with Tears For Fears for 13 years. He has been a lifelong fan of Genesis and highly influenced by Phil Collins and Bill Bruford.

Played on: *Calling All Stations* (four tracks)

Left Genesis: Was only brought in to contribute to the *Calling All Stations* album.

Where is he now: Continues to record and perform (on-and-off) as drummer and lead vocalist for Spock's Beard and is a full-time member of the British prog rock band, Big Big Train, playing drums on eight of their studio albums. Nick lives and works in Fort Wayne, Indiana, where he is the house drummer for Sweetwater Studios.

ANTHONY DRENNAN

Born: 1 November 1958

Place of birth: Luton, Bedfordshire, England

Musical background: Anthony is from a very musical Irish family who returned to Dublin Ireland, when he was very young. His father, Tony, was one of Ireland's most respected jazz pianists and Anthony's two brothers are also well-known jazz musicians. He became a touring guitarist for the Corrs in 1995. Has also regularly played for a number of notable Irish performers including Clannad, Paul Brady and Moving Hearts.

Played on: Didn't play on any Genesis studio recordings but has been a full-time member of Mike and the Mechanics since 2011 and appeared on their last three studio albums.

Left Genesis: Was only brought in for the 'Calling All Stations Tour'.

Where is he now? Based in Dublin, he continues to record and tour with the Corrs and Mike and the Mechanics.

NICK COLLINS

Born: 21 April 2001

Place of birth: Geneva, Switzerland

Musical background: The son of Phil Collins, he started playing drums at a very early age and, in 2015, co-founded the band, Better Strangers, based in Miami, Florida.

Played on: Hasn't played on any Genesis albums but was the drummer for his father's 'Not Dead Yet Tour' in 2017.

Left Genesis: Hasn't had a chance yet!

Where is he now? Took his father's place playing drums to great acclaim on the 'The Last Domino? Tour' from September 2021 through to March 2022.

ABOVE:
Phil Collins, seated on stage due to a neck injury, with son Nick replacing him on drums. 'The Last Domino? Tour', SSE Hydro, Glasgow, October 2021

Released:
March 1969
Label:
Decca
Producer:
John Anthony
Recorded:
Regent Sounds Studio, London, England
UK:
Did not chart
USA:
Did not chart

Side I:

1. Where the Sweet Turns to Sour
2. In the Beginning
3. Firesound Song
4. The Serpent
5. Am I Very Wrong?
6. In the Wilderness

Side 2:

1. The Conqueror
2. In Hiding
3. One Day
4. Window
5. In Limbo
6. Silent Sun
7. A Place to Call My Own

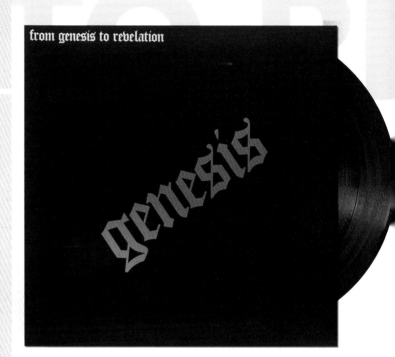

from genesis to revelation

genesis

his debut album from a gang of posh, probably spotty, public schoolboys (some of whom, they admit, really couldn't play their instruments very well) was the result of a school friend being bold enough to leave a demo tape of their nameless band in Jonathan King's car when he returned to his alma mater at Charterhouse for an old boys' day. Surprisingly, he liked it, especially Peter Gabriel's singing voice, and invited them over to a small studio in London's equivalent to Tin Pan Alley in Soho's Denmark Street to record two singles, followed by their first (and could easily have been their last) album. King's influence was minimal and short-lived but he did serve his purpose in gaining them studio experience, coming up with the band's name and correctly pointing out that Chris Stewart was not a great drummer. Jonathan Silver took the stool in May '68 and went on to record all but one of the tracks on this debut album.

GENESIS
VELATION

Most Genesis fans playing it for the first time several years after the band's rise to success would be understandably surprised with what they heard: this is not Genesis! This is an amalgam of Bee Gees warbling, Mellotron drenched Moody Blues and English baroque pop, written by a group of boys who actually wanted to be songwriters rather than performers and, on some of the numbers, are simply obeying Jonathan King's instructions to come up with a short and sharp hit.

It's certainly not a great album – there's so much similarity among many of the songs that, unless you concentrate, it's easy to lose track of which number you're listening to. For many purchasers (and there were only 649 when it was first released), it would have enjoyed one spin on the turntable for each side, then back into the sleeve to be left undisturbed and gathering dust for many years to come. But neither, if you give it another chance, is it a terrible album. Give it a couple more spins and there are one or two impressive aspects that become more apparent.

The opening track, 'Where the Sweet Turns to Sour' is a decent song that already offers hints towards the future of Genesis' keyboard domination and dramatic vocals. Track two, 'In the Beginning' is so Sixties and strongly influenced by early David Bowie and the likes of the English band, Nirvana. 'Fireside Song', with its long piano intro blending into a melody created on 12-string guitars by Phillips and Rutherford, would have been a decent ballad if not drowning in King's overwhelming strings, but again offers some recognition of where they're heading. 'The Serpent', probably the best song on the album, is based around a great little guitar riff that sounds so Al Stewart and could easily be an early Seventies private detective theme tune.

The album does tail off somewhat from this point onwards, and several of the songs are far too long (another pointer towards the future...), but there is, overall, a suggestion of real talent here. These are 17- and 18-year-old schoolboys (Anthony Phillips, regarded as the most gifted at that stage, was actually only 16 when it was recorded) and that should not be forgotten. In less than two years' time, the genuine Genesis will be revealed.

Released:
October 1970
Label:
Charisma
Producer:
John Anthony
Recorded:
Trident Studios, London, England
UK:
98
USA:
Did not chart

Side 1:

1. Looking For Someone
2. White Mountain
3. Visions of Angels

Side 2:

1. Stagnation
2. Dusk
3. The Knife

From *Genesis to Revelation* to this, in less than two years, was a remarkable leap of faith – the result of 22 months of sheer hard work and determination. Here was a band that had matured musically and progressed so far beyond their poppy and rather nondescript debut LP. Once again there'd been a change of drummer when John Silver made the decision to study in America and was replaced by the older and more experienced John Mayhew in August 1969. Genesis turned professional that same month and began working on new material to reflect their belief in more complicated, often intense material, which, at that time, defied definition.

Their first professional performance was in November that year as they embarked on more than a year of daily 10- to 12-hour rehearsals plus regular gigs on the club

and university circuit. Any time off was largely spent listening to LPs, particularly King Crimson's debut album, *In the Court of the Crimson King*. Day by day and week by week, they listened, and learned, and worked on developing their own mystical/folky/proggy/baroque-esque sound that would soon define Genesis. Signed to Charisma Records in 1970, they made their way to Trident Studios in July that year to record *Trespass*, selecting the best of their songs written over the last two years, all of which had been performed live on a regular basis.

The album opens with the superb 'Looking for Someone', which immediately raised eyebrows when heard for the first time in 1970; here was something very different to just about anything else around at the time; Gabriel's vocals and nice flute interludes, disjointed rhythms and Tony Banks's multi-layered, Mellotron-drenched keyboards would help define the Genesis sound over the next seven or eight years.

Better still, it's not the only good track – in fact, there are no poor numbers on *Trespass*. Phillips and Rutherford's 'White Mountain', continues the theme with a song based on Jack London's novel, *White Fang* – the story of a lone wolf engaged in a violent, lupine power struggle. 'Visions of Angels' brings Side 1 to an end, originated from a piano piece written by Phillips during Charterhouse days and rejected for their first album, but re-recorded here very well by John Anthony and dominated once again by Banks's keyboards and the band's strong choral vocals.

'Dusk' – a folky, Strawbs-influenced ballad and the only song on *Trespass* that comes in at under five minutes – bridges the gap very nicely between the two most impressive nine-minutes wonders on Side 2: the complexly structured 'Stagnation' with its one-minute verses interspersed with a three-minute instrumental section before a dramatic vocal and flute crescendo from Peter Gabriel; and, of course, the crowd-pleasing 'The Knife', written by Gabriel and Banks and inspired by Keith Emerson's aggressive keyboard style for Charisma labelmates, the Nice, bringing the album to a dramatic and much harder-edged conclusion.

Throughout the album, Gabriel's singing voice has developed almost beyond recognition and the band's overall harmony vocals (which Jonathan King had encouraged but were clearly beyond them two years earlier) are, at times, superb. Equally important, their musicianship has improved dramatically, particularly Rutherford's bass playing, while the drummer, John Mayhew, deserves recognition for *Trespass*; he's a decent drummer who tends to be overlooked because of who was to take the drum stool next. Ant Phillips is also somewhat underrated (with Steve Hackett waiting in the wings) but he wrote almost half the songs on this album, introduced the band's layered 12-string guitar technique, plays a great solo at the end of 'The Knife' and was a vital element of the band's output and overall sound at that stage.

Trespass sold around 6,000 copies and struggled into the UK charts at No. 98, but is far more than just an indicator of what's to come. It's one of the best Genesis albums in its own right.

Released:
November 1971
Label:
Charisma
Producer:
John Anthony
Recorded:
Trident Studios, London, England
UK:
39
USA:
Did not chart

Side 1:

1. The Musical Box
2. For Absent Friends
3. Return of the Giant Hogweed

Side 2:

1. Seven Stones
2. Harold the Barrel
3. Harlequin
4. The Fountain of Salmacis

With Ant Phillips having left Genesis after taking medical advice, and John Mayhew, due to his drumming style, being asked to make an exit, it was up to Phil Collins and Steve Hackett to fill the gaps. Moving to Tony Stratton Smith's 16th-century property, Luxford House in East Sussex, the band spent three months writing and rehearsing new material in preparation for recording their next album, once again at Trident Studios in London and with John Anthony producing.

Probably no other Genesis album gets off to a better start than *Nursery Cryme* with the lengthy, 10-and-a-half minute, but bizarrely gripping, 'The Musical Box', which describes a macabre Victorian tale of a young boy called Henry who, rather carelessly, is decapitated by his friend Cynthia while playing croquet in the garden.

Cynthia goes back to the house and plays Henry's old musical box, only to be confronted by his spirit as an old man who attempts to seduce her. He's interrupted by the children's nurse who, recognising evil, throws the musical box at the wall and sends Henry's spirit packing. An everyday tale of headless sex, heavy balls and long-handled mallets. The album cover depicting such violent scenes is illustrated by the artist Paul Whitehouse (who had also designed *Trespass*) and is based on the manor house in Chobham, Surrey, where Peter Gabriel had been brought up.

Peter Gabriel had wanted more sex and violence in Genesis music and here, clearly, he'd been successful by contributing dramatically to what had originally been composed by Mike Rutherford and Ant Phillips. Created on 12-string guitars using experimental tunings to create the jangly introduction, 'The Musicial Box' became one of the band's most popular live numbers for years to come. Genesis' interim guitarist, Mick Barnard, who spent a short period with the band before Steve Hackett arrived, also contributed by writing the musical box-effect on guitar that's used repeatedly before the vocal anticipation ("Here it comes again...") that ultimately leads into Hackett's superb guitar solo featuring an early example of fretboard-tapping, popularised by Eddie Van Halen in the late Seventies. It's not a bad way to introduce yourself to Genesis' expanding fan base. 'The Return of the Giant Hogweed', which concludes Side 1 – a warning against the spread of a toxic plant introduced into the UK from Russia by a Victorian explorer – also features Hackett at his best with its fretboard-tapping intro.

Phil Collins's introduction was also pretty impressive with his jazz fusion-influenced drum breaks throughout 'Hogweed' and his rolling drum parts on both that and the middle section of 'The Musical Box'. He also takes lead vocals on the charming, folky 'For Absent Friends',

a one-and-a-half minute Beatle-esque ballad that he and Hackett wrote together and, to their surprise, was happily included on the album. Throughout the album Collins regularly doubles up with Gabriel's vocals and immediately it's clear that there's an uncanny similarity in their voices, which would prove very useful a few years later.

After the brilliant Side 1, there's an element of expectation that Side 2 won't quite live up to it and, sadly, it doesn't. The folky 'Seven Stones' is best appreciated for its nice choral vocals concerning a god who no longer cares; it's a nice enough ballad but never quite fulfils its potential. 'Harold the Barrel' is another example of Collins's early influences, singing the comedy playlet lyric as a duet with Peter Gabriel. There are much better (and worse!) examples to come on future albums. And Mike Rutherford's 'Harlequin' never really gets going before fading away.

The Greek myth-inspired 'The Fountain of Salmacis', written by Tony Banks while at university, originally as a 15-minute musical saga, makes full use of the Mellotron he'd recently purchased from King Crimson. Reduced to eight minutes for the album, it's an interesting piece that climaxes with another excellent Steve Hackett guitar solo, but never quite reaches the heights of the two earlier longer pieces.

Making it to No. 39 in the UK charts, *Nursery Cryme* is a good album that lacks the folkier aspects of *Trespass* and shows signs of chaos in places amongst what is, without the input of Ant Phillips, not their best collection of songs. It rang a few alarm bells for Genesis fans that, even with the impressive performances from two new members, this might be a band that had peaked with its first 'proper' album, and it would be downhill from here. They needn't have worried.

Released:

October 1972

Label:

Charisma

Producer:

Dave Hitchcock and Genesis

Recorded:

Island Studios, London, England

UK:

3

USA:

70

Side I:

1. Watcher of the Skies
2. Time Table
3. Get 'Em Out by Friday
4. Can-Utility and the Coastliners

Side 2:

1. Horizons
2. Supper's Ready

   i.   Lover's Leap

   ii. The Guaranteed Eternal Sanctuary Man

   iii. Ikhnaton and Itsacon and Their Band of Merry Men

   iv. How Dare I Be So Beautiful?

   v. Willow Farm

   vi. Apocalypse in 9/8 (Co-starring the Delicious Talents of Gabbie Ratchet)

   vii. As Sure as Eggs is Eggs (Aching Men's Feet)

The writing and recording of *Foxtrot* took part during a perfect rock music environment for Genesis when several bands decided this was the time not just for long songs, but for really long songs, as prog confirmed its importance within the overall rock music genre. Yes had just released *Close to the Edge*, ELP had gone still further by recording a live LP based on the classical piece *Pictures at an Exhibition* by the Russian composer Modest Mussorgsky, while Jethro Tull came up with a two-sided parody of the concept album, *Thick as a Brick*, with just one piece of music spread across two sides. What could Genesis produce to compete? They didn't quite have the material to go for one track, two sides, but the outstanding number on *Foxtrot*, 'Supper's Ready', a seven-part composition covering themes from religion, mythology and the supernatural, works brilliantly on every level.

The second side opens with 'Horizons', a short classical guitar instrumental performed by Steve Hackett and based on a piece for cello written by J. S. Bach. He didn't expect the band to consider it suitable for the album and was pleasantly surprised when they did, so didn't care too much when many regarded it as just the intro to 'Supper's Ready'. As he said in an interview with *Prog* magazine in 2012, "We came to the conclusion that you could join any two bits of music together, no matter how disparate the styles. We were working on the idea of the musical continuum without naming it as such – it creates for the listener an adventure, an odyssey."

'Supper's Ready' was certainly that. With its theme of good versus evil, this 23-minute masterpiece was inspired partly by an experience of Peter Gabriel's first wife, Jill, while visiting her parents' flat at the Old Barracks in Kensington Palace, London, when the windows blew open and she went into some sort of trance. 'Lover's Leap' opens the song medley with Peter Gabriel's gentle vocal description of the unnerving incident, which he and the band's producer, John Anthony, had both witnessed; it was, said John, some sort of "manifestation" or "psychic phenomenon", while Peter claimed to see "figures in white cloaks" (which are illustrated on the album's front cover). None of them, he claimed, had been drinking or taking any drugs. "It was," he said, "an experience I could not forget and was the starting point for a song about the struggle between good and evil."

No surprise, perhaps, that from that point on, the song suite just extends, keeps going, and going, building and extending, never dragging or flagging, and lays down it cards as one of the finest 20-minute plus pieces of Seventies rock ever. There's a little bit of everything squeezed in, from Beatles-inspired background discussions and weird special effects, knobs and whistles, and four flute solos from Gabriel in between his superb vocals, which seem to have been transported to a whole new level. Mike Rutherford's bass playing and his use of bass pedals, which he'd only recently learned to play, also demonstrate an impressive leap forward in musicianship. Phil Collins's drumming throughout is every bit as impressive as fans had already come to expect and, as for Tony Banks, do we even need to mention his supreme keyboard and Mellotron playing that dominates this long piece and much of the album overall?

The band were almost certainly responding to pressure from Charisma Records that they should come up with much bigger album sales for the company than the three previous LPs, none of which had fulfilled their financial promise. Written over the summer of 1972 and combining songs that had already been performed live with new material worked out during rehearsals in London, recording got underway at Island Studios in August. Once again, John Anthony initially took the helm as producer but, following disagreements with the band, was subsequently replaced with two new names, co-producer Dave Hitchcock and sound engineer John Barnes, who would go on to produce the next three Genesis albums.

Among a collection of songs in which none are weak, and all combine to create something exceptional, the opening track, 'Watcher of the Skies', is another hugely impressive long piece at seven-and-a-half minutes and one of the two songs the band had been playing live for some time. Based on Keat's sonnet 'On First Looking into Chapman's Homer' written in 1816, an Arthur C. Clarke novel *Childhood's End*, combined with a Marvel Comics story theme, it asks questions concerning what aliens watching from afar would make of us as we continued to destroy the Earth.

'Get 'Em Out by Friday' is another of the album's genuinely great numbers, described by Gabriel as "part social comment, part prophetic" concerning disadvantaged people being evicted from tower blocks by greedy landlords, partly inspired by his own problems at his flat in Islington, north London. It's one of the early Genesis songs featuring several characters, each with a different voice that Peter vocalises accordingly, and believably, well. With such diversity, dense lyrics and comedic elements, it wasn't easy for

Gabriel to nail it in the studio, let alone live, but he succeeds in creating one of the album's highlights.

The two remaining numbers on Side 1 – 'Time Table', written by Tony Banks with a romantic theme celebrating older times and traditional values – and 'Can-Utility and the Coastliners' – the other song already played live during a brief Italian tour – is based on a similar apocryphal theme illustrating King Canute's humility as he fails to hold back the tide. Neither are among the album's standout tracks, but nor are they lightweight pop songs; both are very listenable and enjoyable and bring Side 1 to an end in preparation for their Magnum Opus, 'Supper's Ready'.

The album's infamous cover was the last of the three Genesis LPs designed by Paul Whitehead, a rather strange amalgam of images inspired by Peter Gabriel's lyrics. Not liked at all by the band, the cover is generally regarded, nonetheless, as one of the most dramatic and best-known album covers of all time. Just like the album itself, everything about *Foxtrot* is unforgettable.

Peter Gabriel wearing the infamous red dress and foxhead costume
at Newcastle City Hall, October 1972

Released:
October 1973
Label:
Charisma
Producer:
Genesis and John Burns
Recorded:
Island Studios, London, England
UK:
3
USA:
70

Side I:

1. Dancing With the Moonlit Knight
2. I Know What I Like (In Your Wardrobe)
3. Firth of Fifth
4. More Fool Me

Side 2:

1. The Battle of Epping Forest
2. After the Ordeal
3. The Cinema Show
4. Aisle of Plenty

GENESIS

SELLING ENGLAND BY THE POUND

Following their first major tour in the USA, Charisma put the band under considerable pressure to release new material to capitalise on the commercial success of both *Foxtrot* (a No. 1 album in Italy) and the budget-priced album *Genesis Live* that had made it to No. 9 in the UK. There'd been very little chance to write new material while travelling around the States and the band found themselves with less than three months (and a stingy budget of just £13,000) to write and record a new album.

Having rehearsed and written sufficient material at locations in Chessington and London's Shepherd Bush, the band entered Island Studios, London in August 1973 with John Burns – sound engineer on *Foxtrot* – brought in to help as co-producer. The title, it had been decided, would be *Selling England by the Pound*, purported to have been taken from a Labour Party slogan in its manifesto protesting against increased American commercialisation and its effect on traditional English culture. (It appears, however, that no Labour Party manifesto has ever included that phrase or anything similar. It's more likely to have come from one of the Party's smaller publications around that time.)

'Dancing with the Moonlit Knight' is one of the band's best ever opening tracks – made up of several of Peter Gabriel's short piano pieces combined with some of Steve Hackett's pastoral, folk guitar pieces. Gabriel added English-themed lyrics (the two opening lines sung *a cappella*: "Can you tell me where my country lies, said the unifaun to his true love's eyes") in an effort to reject any suggestions that the band had sold out to America. And although Steve Hackett had not contributed a great deal of material at this stage, his guitar solo (one of many impressive examples on this album) is considered by many to be his best during his time with Genesis.

Such a blistering opener is followed by the equally quintessentially English but dramatically effective 'I Know What I Like (In Your Wardrobe)', also based on one of Hackett's guitar pieces and put together during an improvisation session in London. It was from this track that the LP cover was derived; the painting entitled *The Dream,* by the artist, Betty Swanwick, already existed but, at the band's request, she added the image of a lawn mower, mentioned three times in the song lyric. It became the first Genesis single to enter the UK chart, climbing to No. 21.

A great start, but the quality continues with Tony Banks's 'Firth of Fifth', made up of three separate piano pieces originally rejected for *Foxtrot*, but then reworked for *Selling England by the Pound*; it's a beautiful piece of music, highlighted once again by a Hackett solo that possibly even betters his effort on the opening track. To bring to an end what is arguably the best single side of any of their albums, Rutherford and Collins contributed the romantic ballad 'More Fool Me' – only the second time Phil Collins took lead vocals before his change of role in 1975.

Side 2 opens with 'The Battle of Epping Forest', another of Peter Gabriel's musical playlets, inspired by a newspaper story he'd spotted several years earlier regarding East End gangland

fights in Epping Forest, bordering northeast London. Unable to find the piece again in library archives, he eventually just made up his own characters (such as 'The Bethnal Green Butcher') in a comedic but, at almost 12 minutes, very lengthy piece that just about manages to maintain its grasp on the listener's attention.

'After the Ordeal' is an instrumental written by Hackett, introduced with an acoustic guitar and piano before yet another of his excellent guitar solos, but it's 'The Cinema Show' that many consider the best track on the LP. With its slow, two-minute, 12-string guitar intro (retuned to harmonics) before picking up the pace, an instrumental section from Gabriel on flute and oboe followed by an uncannily Crosby, Stills and Nash vocal harmony middle eight before, once again, Steve Hackett's unique guitar sound combined with Tony Banks's extended keyboard solo. The album closes with a segue into 'Aisle of Plenty', a reprise of the opening track having a final stab at consumerism by ridiculing tacky sales techniques of British supermarkets inherited from American forerunners.

Lyrically or musically there's nothing that could be described as easy-listening on this impressive Genesis LP, although it does, perhaps, at times, sound a little spiritless – cruising along the middle of dappled English country lanes, lacking the same level of angst and aggression in comparison to its predecessor.

As always, the media and public reviews were mixed: "the band's best, most adventurous album to date", stated *New Musical Express*; "indistinctive and tedious" was the opinion of the *Guardian*; "less black humour and more ethereal" said *Melody Maker*. Charisma's Tony Stratton Smith was disappointed because of what he considered too many instrumental sections. Perhaps a more important opinion from the band's point of view was that of the Beatles' John Lennon, who mentioned in an interview how much he liked the album. Steve Hackett (understandably) regards it as his favourite Genesis record, but Banks and Rutherford (equally understandably!) both expressed mixed feelings; Banks, in particular, was unhappy about the number of tracks on the LP, which affected the overall sound quality. Perhaps, for their next effort, there would be only one obvious conclusion – a double album.

Released:
November 1974
Label:
Charisma
Producer:
Genesis and John Burns
Recorded:
Glaspant Manor, Camarthenshire, Wales
UK:
10
USA:
41

Side 1:

1. The Lamb Lies Down on Broadway
2. Fly on a Windscreen
3. Broadway Melody of 1974
4. Cuckoo Cocoon
5. In the Cage
6. The Grand Parade of Lifeless Packaging

Side 2:

1. Back in NYC
2. Hairless Heart
3. Counting Out Time
4. Carpet Crawlers
5. The Chamber of 32 Doors

Side 3:

1. Lilywhite Lilith
2. The Waiting Room
3. Anyway
4. Here Comes the Supernatural Anaesthetist
5. The Lamia
6. Silent Sorrow in Empty Boats

Side 4:

1. The Colony of Slippermen
   i.   The Arrival
   ii. A Visit to the Doktor
   iii. The Raven
2. Ravine
3. The Light Dies Down on Broadway
4. Riding the Scree
5. In the Rapids
6. It

After a nine-month, back-breaking tour across Europe, the UK, Canada and the USA from September '73 to May '74 to support *Selling England by the Pound,* Genesis returned to the UK and almost immediately moved en masse into Headley Grange in Hampshire to work on new material for three months. Already, given how much had been crammed onto their last LP, the decision had been made that their next album should be a double concept album. Initially Mike Rutherford came up with the idea of basing the concept on Antoine de Saint-Exupéry's 1943 children's fable *The Little Prince* but Peter Gabriel thought that was too simplistic. He wanted to tell his tale of a Puerto Rican street kid, called Rael, in New York City, who sets out on an adventure where he will meet strange characters and weird situations along the way.

Loosely based on the book (Arthur Laurents) and musical (Leonard Bernstein/Stephen Sondheim) *West Side Story* (itself inspired by Shakespeare's *Romeo and Juliet*) and Alejandro Jodorowsky's Mexican avant-garde Western, *El Topo*, Gabriel's concept wasn't exactly embraced by the other members of the band. All had their own personal problems at that time and the tension levels were high, particularly Peter's, whose wife, Jill, was in hospital going through a very difficult pregnancy. While Peter worked alone on the album's lyrics, most of the songs were developed by the rest of the band through improvisation and recorded at Glaspant Manor in Wales, using Island Record's mobile studio.

Gabriel found himself under so much pressure that, reluctantly, he had to ask Banks and Rutherford to help out with some of the words. With assistance from co-producer John Burns, the backing tracks for the entire album were completed within two weeks but Gabriel was still working on the lyrics a month later. So frantic did it become to make their deadline that, in September '74, the band relocated to Island Studios in London and began working on 24-hour sessions, with Collins mixing and dubbing all night before Tony and Mike would take over during the day.

Working on the album proved to be a painful experience and two of the band members were far from happy when it was released in November. Tony Banks described it as "of all my time in Genesis, my least favourite period"; no surprise the album does not feature in his list of the Top 10 Genesis albums. Rutherford found it equally frustrating: "It lacked cohesion. It was a wonderful journey, but I feel that a conversation should be able to be explained in one long sentence or in a paragraph and you can't really do that with *The Lamb Lies Down on Broadway*."

Trying to assess it coherently is equally difficult. The simple way is just to play the first disc from start to finish; from 'The Lamb Lies Down on Broadway' through to 'The Chamber of 32 Doors', this is a stunning album. Not one second of any of the individual songs is anything less than breathtaking; play them through non-stop in sequence, and they're better still.

Move on to Side 3 and here's where the picky problems (such as they are) begin. The concept loses its way somewhat and the second disc could, maybe, have benefitted from some pruning. Peter Gabriel had actually suggested that the album should be released as two separate LPs about six months apart, but nobody was interested. A better idea might have been a three-sided LP; it wouldn't have been the first – Johnny Winter's *Second Winter* had been released in that format in 1969. One of those ideas might have won more support from critics and plenty of disgruntled fans. There was a bumpy ride ahead.

Gabriel had been concerned from the outset that the album's critical reception wouldn't be good and might lead to a negative backlash. They certainly got one. *NME* described the album as "having to wade across a ploughed field in wellies to reach the hedge on the other side"; while *Melody Maker* felt the album was "lacking in character, as they plod through the arrangements, with little fire or purpose". Before its release, Genesis set across North America and Europe to perform the album in its entirety to an audience that had never heard it, combined with a complicated multi-media stage show that regularly went wrong; understandably, the response was mixed.

Interesting, but not unexpected, that something this good could be criticised so harshly... the difficult double album: the Beatles 'White Album', the Rolling Stones *Exile on Main Street*, Fleetwood Mac's *Tusk* – trash then, but treasure now. Despite the levels of stress it created among the band, *The Lamb Lies Down on Broadway* carpet-crawled its way through piles of criticism before making it to the other side to be hailed a work of genius. These days, it's an album that regularly makes it into the Top 10 'best progressive rock albums of all time' polls.

Just six days into the supporting tour, on 20 November 1974, Peter Gabriel announced to the band in Cleveland, Ohio, that he would leave Genesis once the tour was completed. This, Gabriel's swansong, was a good one with which to depart. He told *Prog* magazine in 2012: "I'm not sure if the story made much sense to most people, but it did mean something to me; in essence, it was something about an awakening. He [Rael] was on a journey to find himself in a seductive, magical place." Peter had taken his own leap into the unknown. The band's came next.

Released:
February 1976
Label:
Charisma
Producer:
David Hentschel and Genesis
Recorded:
Trident Studios, London, England
UK:
3
USA:
31

Side 1:

1. Dance on a Volcano
2. Entangled
3. Squonk
4. Mad Man Moon

Side 2:

1. Robbery, Assault and Battery
2. Ripples
3. A Trick of the Tail
4. Los Endos

How do you replace such a creative talent as Peter Gabriel? The answer is, don't try. What about the vocals? Again, no need to worry. Phil Collins's contributions to the previous four studio albums, twinning vocals with Gabriel as well as drumming brilliantly, were far more important than anyone had appreciated. And the wonderful (if slowly declining in interest) Steve Hackett (who had just recorded his first solo album *Voyage of the Acolyte*) is still behind the guitar, so why are there any concerns that this won't be a great album?

It's never easy losing your star player, which Gabriel was, but in some ways his departure made life easier for the others. His forcible dominance of *The Lamb Lies Down on Broadway* and insistence on those bizarre costumes and unnerving stage characters didn't always go down well with his colleagues; there were times when it caused chaos.

Tony Banks was the band member who'd been closest to Peter but was also the most determined to carry on, even if it meant donating towards a new Genesis album some of his best material pigeonholed for a planned solo project, just to prove they could survive without him. It's one of the most impressive crops of Banks songs, being credited on all eight tracks, and all very impressive (bar one).

For fans, it must have been a huge relief to discover, when hearing the opening song, 'Dance of the Volcano' for the first time, that it was hard to detect it wasn't Peter Gabriel singing. Perhaps it was? No, they didn't need him any more. Like it or not, this was the way Genesis intended to progress. And what's not to like? 'Entangled', written largely by Steve Hackett and composed by Banks, is even better and suddenly everything sounds like *Selling England by the Pound* once again, despite that troublesome *The Lamb Lies Down On Broadway*. 'Entangled' is a superb piece of music with its spooky theme of an English children's music box, which could easily have found its way onto *The Shining* soundtrack a few years later.

This is great stuff, but will it begin to fade? Not at all. Up next is 'Squonk', written by Rutherford and Banks based on a hunter who captures a mythical creature;

a hard-edged number with its Led Zeppelin 'Kashmir'-inspired repetitive riff. That's 19 minutes in for Side 1, which most bands would think sufficient, but they're not done. What follows is the longest song so far 'Mad Man Moon', inspired by William Golding's novel *The Inheritors* about an extinct alien race, expressed as a romantic ballad. But it works!

All of the songs are six-minutes plus, apart from the title track, and there's not one bad number; the only element of weakness is the somewhat irritating 'Robbery, Assault and Battery' to open Side 2, with its fey-cockney attempt to compete with 'Battle of Epping Forest' but failing to match a song that wasn't everyone's cup of Rosy Lee on *Selling England by the Pound* anyway. The three remaining songs are all far more memorable: the eight-minute 'Ripples' with its lovely sing-a-long chorus; superb Beatles-esque 'A Trick of the Tail'; and, bringing it all to a very satisfying conclusion, the instrumental band written 'Los Endos', paying respect to the other collective composition 'Dance on a Volcano' that got things going 51 enjoyable minutes earlier.

Fans and critics loved it. A great album. Great songs. Great lyrics. Great cover by Colin Elgie at Hipgnosis. Superb production by David Hentschel. And great vocals by Phil Collins. Together, they'd proved they could survive without him. The King is dead. Long live the King. (Not Jonathan.)

Released:
December 1976
Label:
Charisma/Atco
Producer:
David Hentschel and Genesis
Recorded:
Relight Studios, Hilvarenbeek, Netherlands
UK:
7
USA:
26

Side I:

1. Dance on a Volcano
2. Entangled
3. Squonk
4. Mad Man Moon

Side 2:

1. All in a Mouse's Night
2. Blood on the Rooftops
3. Unquiet Slumber for the Sleepers...
4. ...In That Quiet Earth
5. Afterglow

Wind & Wuthering is the best of the Genesis albums that tend to get sidelined, despite its transitional importance. It was the first Genesis record to be recorded abroad, in Holland, and the last to benefit from Steve Hackett's considerable guitar skills. Most obviously, it was the second album released minus Peter Gabriel and, although the band had proved they could survive without him, the question was, could they do it again?

Punk had already arrived on the UK shores by mid-'76 and the so-called dinosaurs were already looking over their shoulders without admitting any major concerns. As Phil Collins put it: "They're not talking about us. They're talking about those other bands that I don't like either."

This was probably the last Genesis album that didn't make any compromises, even if from now on they'd need to distance themselves from the sci-fi and fantasy themes for which they were renowned. For *Wind & Wuthering* their choice of subject matter included Emily Brontë's *Wuthering Heights*, from which the album's title and cover was inspired. Other literary connections included Michael Moorcock's sci-fi novel *Phoenix in Obsidian*, while the dramatic, bass-dominated, opening track 'Eleventh Earl of Mar' is based on a historic novel *The Flight of the Heron* by DK Broster, set during the 1745 Jacobite rebellion. As punks approached rattling their belt chains, one can't help but wonder if Genesis weren't cruisin' for a bruisin'.

'One for the Vine' is another impressive 10-minute progger's delight – initially a slow ballad that manages to hold the listener's interest right through to 4.40 minutes when the up-tempo section kicks in. 'Your Own Special Way' is written by Mike Rutherford and clearly signposts his future both with Genesis and with his side-project, Mike and the Mechanics. A basic love song with some laid-back, Clapton-sounding guitar from Steve Hackett throughout, it was picked up by radio stations across America and resulted in listeners reassessing their interpretation of the Genesis sound.

Perhaps less appealing was 'Wot Gorilla' – one of Phil Collins's favourite numbers inspired by his own side-project with jazz-influenced Brand X; it certainly demonstrates his terrific drumming capabilities, but not a lot else. Its selection in preference to Steve Hackett's more interesting 'Please Don't Touch' (the title track of his second solo album) was a key factor in his decision to leave once *Wind & Wuthering* was completed. His frustration at having so many numbers rejected in favour of Tony Banks's material (six credits from nine tracks) is understandable; Hackett had just four, but three of those are among the best songs on the album.

Opening Side 2 is 'All in a Mouse's Night' another melodrama about a little mouse on the run in a house dominated by a large cat; there's an interesting sort of stage musical feel about this almost seven-minute piece, but probably not the ideal number to begin the second side. A much better choice would have been 'Blood on the Rooftops', written by Steve Hackett and Phil Collins and one of the best tracks on the album, featuring Hackett's cynical lyrics conveying his concerns about junk television and its impact on our perception of more important world issues.

'Unquiet Slumbers for the Sleepers... ' / ' ...In that Quiet Earth' are two linked instrumental numbers opening with Hackett's pleasant, ethereal guitar piece with its 'world music' feel leading into Banks's aggressive keyboard link before 'Afterglow', which brings it all to its conclusion. Another Banks composition, 'Afterglow' can also lay claim to the prize as the album's most memorable number. Great melody, great hooks and, as Chris Welch described it in *Melody Maker*, "the stuff of which encores are made".

Surprisingly, neither Rutherford or Collins are big fans of *Wind & Wuthering* but Hackett and Banks have both named it as one of their top three Genesis records. "We brought back the melodrama and straight emotion that we had on some of those earlier albums," said Tony. "I would put 'Blood on the Rooftops' and 'Afterglow' among our best-ever tracks."

The album also received positive reviews from the press, despite how quickly so many had jumped on the now wave bandwagon. *Sounds* summed it up as "less immediate but more substantial" than *A Trick of the Tail; Circus* magazine described the album as "flawless"; while *New Musical Express*, on the other hand, said, "Nobody could call it stimulating – derivative and listless as it is."

Horses for courses, as always. It's certainly not their best LP, but neither is it way down their playlist either, and deserves several listens to appreciate its many attributes before reaching any conclusion. It's worth the effort.

Released:
March 1978
Label:
Charisma/Atlantic
Producer:
David Hentschel and Genesis
Recorded:
Relight Studios, Hilvarenbeek, Netherlands
UK:
3
USA:
23

Side 1:

1. Down and Out
2. Undertow
3. Ballad of Big
4. Snowbound
5. Burning Rope

Side 2:

1. Deep in the Motherlode
2. Many Too Many
3. Scenes From a Night's Dream
4. Say it's Alright Joe
5. The Lady Lies
6. Follow You Follow Me

A s that time when Peter Gabriel had made his move two years earlier, and Steve Hackett followed him down to the unemployment office in August 1977, the remaining three band members (and many fans) were concerned as to where this would lead. The correct answer, as far as this album is concerned – and all three agree – was not in the right direction. That was the case until an unexpected hit single, 'Follow You Follow Me', rescued commercially an album that was, overall, something of a let down.

There was no doubt that Steve Hackett had been missed, and it shows; despite his contributions never being the most prominent aspect of any Genesis album, they were so very important. At that stage, Mike Rutherford was a skilled chordal guitarist and a superb bass player, but not good enough as a lead guitarist

THEN THERE
THREE

and he knew it. Tony Banks also acknowledged that in Steve Hackett he had lost an ally who had encouraged him to explore some weird musical locations that, otherwise, he would not have discovered.

One aspect they had all agreed was that they wanted the new album to reflect the new wave music scene by featuring more concise and less proggy songs, allowing them to include more material. Ironically, 'Follow You Follow Me' was originally intended to be a longer number but was recognised by Atlantic Records as a potential hit single and, as a result, edited for the album. It reached No. 7 in the UK and No. 23 in the USA, making it by far their most successful single to date. As Tony Banks said, "Suddenly we were on radio and people couldn't ignore us."

Banks and Rutherford were the dominant songwriters on '...And Then There Were Three...' with seven songs between them; Collins's contributions to this album were fairly minimal. 'Down and Out' was written collectively during rehearsals, with lyrics from Collins concerning US record labels' lack of respect for musicians. It's a good opening track in terms of its quiet intro being blown apart by a heavy, Sex Pistols-sounding, guitar and synthesizer riff played over some of Collins's most impressive frenetic drumming.

Tony Banks's song, 'Undertow', is a nice ballad that desperately needed a Steve Hackett solo; with it, the song would have slotted perfectly onto Wind & Wuthering, but here seems rather bland. Frustratingly, the same could be said of much of what remains on Side 1. It's difficult, for example, to play 'Snowbound' without thinking of Aled Jones on Christmas morning.

Banks's 'Burning Rope', carries on in much the same vein before almost drifting away until Rutherford's reasonable guitar solo revives things sufficiently to bring Side 1 to a conclusion. Both melodically and lyrically,the album never really gets up and running until Side 2 with 'Deep in the Motherlode' but even then it takes a while to get into its stride and demonstrate Genesis' intended direction for the future.

'Many Too Many' is a good ballad with a hooky chorus; 'Scenes from a Night's Dream', inspired by the American cartoon character, Little Nemo, sounds Rush-influenced and isn't bad but could do without the harmonies; 'Say It's Alright Joe' is another decent ballad about a heavy drinker's broken relationship; 'The Lady Lies', a mystical tale of a man who rescues an evil woman, is also a very catchy number with a hooky chorus; and great bass playing by Mike Rutherford on both of those tracks before 'Follow You Follow Me' is unveiled.

As often the case, newspaper critics' reviews were fairly split down the middle: Melody Maker praised the album as being "as good as any they have made in the band's post-Gabriel years". Village Voice was of the opinion that "without Steve Hackett, the band loses its last remaining focal point". While The Morning News sat on the fence with the conclusion that the album sounded little different to Wind & Wuthering.

That's the reality: play this straight after Wind & Wuthering and you're likely to be slightly disappointed. Play it straight after Abacab and you might be of the opinion that this is a pretty good album after all. Because it is, but just doesn't really go anywhere very exciting.

Released:
March 1980
Label:
Charisma/Atlantic
Producer:
David Hentschel and Genesis
Recorded:
Polar Studios, Stockholm, Sweden
UK:
1
USA:
11

Side 1:

1. Behind the Lines
2. Duchess
3. Guide Vocal
4. Man of Our Times
5. Misunderstanding
6. Heathaze

Side 2:

1. Turn it On Again
2. Alone Tonight
3. Cul-de-Sac
4. Please Don't Ask
5. Duke's Travels
6. Duke's End

I f Genesis had demonstrated on their previous album *...And Then There Were Three...* that they could write a decent pop song, *Duke* is where they did it better still and proved they could do it pretty much whenever they needed to. The album followed another period of inactivity mainly due to the effect that lengthy touring had had on Phil Collins's personal life. Having moved to Vancouver, Canada, at the end of the last world tour in an effort to save his first marriage (while Banks and Rutherford recorded solo albums), Collins returned to England in April '79 when his efforts had failed and began writing a plethora of emotional material, some of which appeared on his first album, *Face Value*.

In the autumn of '79, Banks and Rutherford moved in with Collins at his home in Shalford, Surrey, to begin rehearsals for the new album in his bedroom, and it was decided that each of them should contribute two personal songs while the band would work on the remaining tracks together in the usual method of jamming during rehearsals. Banks offered 'Heathaze' and 'Cul-de-Sac', Rutherford 'Man of Our Times' and 'Alone Tonight', while Collins contributed 'Misunderstanding' and 'Please Don't Ask'. None stood out particularly apart from Collins's 'Misunderstanding' inspired by songs from the Beach Boys, Joe Walsh and Toto, which went on to achieve reasonable success as the third single from *Duke*. Certainly Phil Collins's singing had improved considerably since their last album and the emotion in his voice is there for all to hear. "I'd become a songwriter," said Phil, "and more of a singer because I was singing songs that I'd written."

The first and most successful single from *Duke*, of course, was 'Turn it On Again', which was Genesis' second single to make it into the UK Top 10. In its original form, 'Turn it On Again' and the other remaining five tracks were intended to be a single 30-minute song suite called 'Duke' with six sections combined to tell the tale of a fictional character called Albert, but the idea was eventually dropped to avoid any comparison

with 'Supper's Ready' from *Foxtrot,* and to allow two of those six songs to be released as singles. 'Turn it On Again' was originally planned as a short interlude before 'Duke's Travels'. It's interesting to play those six tracks through in that order, which could have worked perfectly well but would have left Side 2 very ballad-heavy. (The cover art for *Duke*, incidentally, was put together by the French illustrator Lionel Koechlin from his 1979 book *L'Alphabet d'Albert*, of which all three band members were admirers, but there doesn't seem to be any connection between the characters called 'Albert' in both the book and the 'Duke' suite.)

Somewhat surprisingly, *Duke* is Tony Banks's favourite Genesis album. "It's got such a positive quality about it," he says, "One of the strongest moments in Genesis music." Critics agreed, up to a point, and were reassuringly positive in their comments: "no Genesis fan could be disappointed" concluded *Sounds*; the *Los Angeles Times* described the album as identifiably Genesis, but toned-down"; while AllMusic felt the 'Duke' suite maintained "a heavy dose" of progressive rock, an opinion with which many diehard Genesis fans would concur. For them, at least, *Duke* was the last Genesis album that could claim a "heavy dose" of anything similar.

Released:
September 1981
Label:
Charisma/Atlantic
Producer:
Genesis
Recorded:
The Farm, Chiddingfold, Surrey, England
UK:
1
USA:
7

Side 1:

1. Abacab
2. No Reply at All
3. Me and Sarah Jane
4. Keep it Dark

Side 2:

1. Dodo/Lurker
2. Who Dunnit?
3. Man on the Corner
4. Like It or Not
5. Another Record

he first Genesis album recorded at the Farm (although initially written in the farmhouse while the studio was being constructed) *Abacab* got underway in March 1981 but was recorded in the shadow of Phil Collins's *Face Value*, which had climbed to No. 1 in the UK charts and No. 7 in the USA just one month earlier. The new studio environment had a positive effect on the band's songwriting output which, although not dramatically altered, re-focussed on developing new ideas in contrast to the established norm. First and foremost, owning their own recording studio meant they didn't need to worry so much about costs and could, within reason, take their time.

Replacing David Hentschel on the producer's desk was engineer Hugh Padgham, chosen as a result of his

ACAB

work with Phil Collins on *Face Value* and well-known as the man who, almost by accident, had created the gated-reverb effect on Collins's drums, most famously recognised on his hit single 'In the Air Tonight'. When the other members of Genesis heard the difference it made, they immediately wanted Padgham to incorporate the gated-reverb effect on *Abacab*. Happy to oblige, it was also agreed that they should simplify everything by scaling down the keyboard arrangements and the number of overdubs. As Phil Collins put it: "We were trying to reinvent ourselves because punk had left some mark."

Punk had left its mark on just about everyone by 1981, but not always for the better. When they first played the new track 'Who Dunnit?' live at a gig in Holland, they didn't exactly invite their audience to spit at them but they seemed to be encouraging booing, and that's what they got. It was, said Tony Banks, a 'real one-off piece'. Around the world one could hear the mumbled response, "Thank God." It's one of those Beatles 'No. 9' moments but much, much, worse.

Five of the tracks on *Abacab* are group written with the remaining three credited to one each: the reggae influenced 'Me and Sarah Jane' from Banks; the ballad 'Like It or Not' from Rutherford; and Collins's 'Man on the Corner', one of three singles taken from *Abacab*. An edited version of the title song was the most successful of the singles, making it to No. 9 in the UK charts. Based on three sections of music – A, B and C – originally used to construct the number in the sequence A-B-A-C-A-B (although the finished song isn't!), it's probably standout track among the album's rather disappointing overall collection.

Close second are 'Keep It Dark', retracing Genesis' earlier fascination with sci-fi themes with its tale of a man transported to an alien planet, and the Side 2 opener 'Dodo'/'Lurker' – a funky number that takes a respectable backward step towards the longer, keyboard-drenched numbers with which Banks dominated Genesis back in the '70s. It's not bad but, like most of the rest of *Abacab*, doesn't really grab you by ... anything. It's unfortunate (the spoken section particularly) as this could have been the best track on the album if (even if only on this one number) they had denied another passage of transition and stuck to what they did so well just a few years earlier.

Melody Maker considered the album the band's "least consistent and therefore, least predictable release of the last three years", but concluded, "far more promising" than the previous two albums. Others such as the *Los Angeles Times* raised the question as to how much the success of Collins's *Face Value* and its enormous drum sound had influenced the band. It was a question that didn't need to be asked.

Released:
October 1983
Label:
Charisma/Virgin/Atlantic
Producer:
Genesis and Hugh Padgham
Recorded:
The Farm, Chiddingfold, Surrey, England
UK:
1
USA:
9

Side I:

1. Mama
2. That's All
3. Home By the Sea
4. Second Home By the Sea

Side 2:

1. Illegal Alien
2. Taking it All Too Hard
3. Just a Job to Do
4. Silver Rainbow
5. It's Gonna Get Better

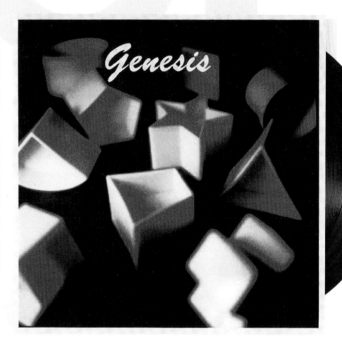

A t last, their ambition had been fulfilled: the Farm was up and running and open for business. They owned their own recording studio close to all three band members' homes in leafy Surrey; now they could write, rehearse, record and mix all in the same place and be home in time for tea.

New wave music had undoubtedly had an affect on Genesis and most other so-called rock dinosaurs; with the weight of punk on their posh, polo-shirted shoulders, here was a chance to start again, in their own studio, and create a new album for Genesis fans old and new. Here was their opportunity, many believed, for them to produce another proper, enthralling Genesis LP that would be a big improvement over the disappointing *Abacab*. So did they? Hmmmm...

Commercially, at least, they succeeded: *Genesis* was a Top 10 LP in both the UK (with sales of 600,000) and the USA (over 4 million sales), with no less than five singles taken from it, but in terms of its creativity and artistic prowess, it's another album that failed to tick all the boxes and left many loyal fans disappointed once again.

The seemingly rather lazy title *Genesis* was chosen because it reflected their feelings that this was a new Genesis, in their own studio, and that this album was all written collectively by the three of them. The opening song, 'Mama', was originally planned to be the album title but, after consideration, they felt it would draw too much attention to just one song (despite having done so several times before on previous albums).

'Mama' came about as a result of Mike Rutherford experimenting with a drum machine played through the now infamous gated-reverb at such a level of volume that the speaker cabinets began vibrating across the studio floor. With lyrics from Collins, it explores the feelings of a young man obsessed with desire for an older prostitute. It was also Phil who came up with the idea of that rather unsettling laugh inspired by the song 'The Master' from the US rapper band Grandmaster Flash and the Furious Five. It works well for a black rapper but not so sure for Phil, always makes me wonder if he's about to be sick. Whatever, released as a single, 'Mama' was their first Top 5 hit in the UK, although it only made it to No. 73 in the USA.

'That's All' is probably the best track on the album, a memorable, Beatles-esque, hooky-filled pop single that made it to No. 6 in the US to become their biggest hit single so far. Phil's drumming style on the song is in tribute to one of his heroes, the Beatles' Ringo Starr. 'Home By the Sea' is not far behind in terms of its drum-bombarded funky rhythms making use of Phil's first electronic drum kit. 'Second Home by the Sea', however (basically a predominantly 6-minutes instrumental continuation of 'Home by the Sea') is OK but another classic Hugh Padgham drum-fest that drags on until Phil's vocals return with a minute or so left to run.

Then we arrive at the Side 2 opener, 'Illegal Alien' which is, let's face it, pretty awful. According to Phil Collins it's a tongue-in-cheek look at the issues of Mexican immigrants attempting to cross the US border illegally. Hilarious. Like 10cc but minus anything remotely funny. Nothing else leaps out on Side 2, or at least, thankfully, not as bad as that. 'It's Gonna Get Better', with its sampled intro taken from a classical piece for the cello, brings *Genesis* to a conclusion quite nicely, although it's hard, if you close your eyes, not to envisage a boy band trying to look enigmatic while gliding across the stage.

Genesis is certainly the band's most obvious declaration that future material will be dominated by shorter and simpler radio-friendly numbers, and that any sign of prog influences would be much harder to discern. Mike Rutherford said he considers this one of their best ever albums, particularly Side 1. "Good mix of long songs and short songs," he sums it up rather simplistically; no in-depth analysis (or jacket) required. What do I know?

Upon its release, Genesis became the band's third album in succession to reach No. 1 in the UK charts and No. 9 in the US Hot 100. In 1985 the album was nominated for a Grammy Award for 'Best Rock Performance' while 'Second Home by the Sea' was up for 'Best Rock Instrumental Performance'. Rather surprisingly, it's *Kerrang!* Magazine that concludes: "A Genesis album for people who normally hate Genesis... great music for the masses." It's hard not to agree.

Released:
June 1986
Label:
Charisma/Virgin/Atlantic
Producer:
Genesis and Hugh Padgham
Recorded:
Relight Studios, Hilvarenbeek, Netherlands
UK:
1
USA:
3

Side I:

1. Invisible Touch
2. Tonight, Tonight, Tonight
3. Land of Confusion
4. In Too Deep

Side 2:

1. Anything She Does
2. Domino
   Part One – In the Glow of the Night
   Part Two – The Last Domino
3. Throwing it All Away
4. The Brazilian

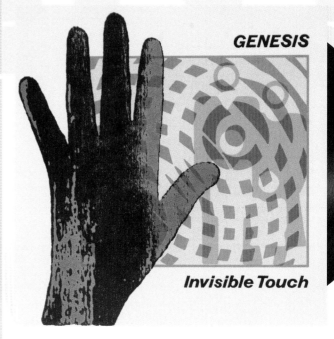

GENESIS

Invisible Touch

Following another year's solo work, Genesis reconvened at the Farm studio in September 1985 to write and record their new album with co-producer/engineer Hugh Padgham at the controls, seemingly with the intention on creating Genesis' biggest ever overproduced and drum-overloaded album. Phil Collins had something of an obsession with Prince (not Charles) at the time and had just acquired a Simmons electronic drum kit, which may have had a lot to do with it... The band then used the electronic kit with which to compose their music, but it definitely had a dramatic effect on their unusual and much-anticipated time signatures and tempo changes.

As before, the band entered the studio with no properly formed ideas other than developing songs through jamming and improvisation, which would be recorded onto cassette tape. Phil Collins, as the "keeper of the tapes", would then analyse what they had before "chopping away, fine-tuning and honing down all these ideas", or sometimes suggesting bits of music that could be pieced together. As the music progressed, Collins would put words to the tunes off the top of his head until the music had been recorded, with each band member then being responsible for their share of the final lyrics. Phil Collins wrote the words for 'Invisible Touch', 'Tonight, Tonight, Tonight', and 'In Too Deep'; Rutherford 'Land of Confusion' and 'Throwing it All Away'; while Banks was responsible for 'Domino' and 'Anything She Does'.

'Domino' is the track that rescues an album which tends, in places, to drift into the middle of the road. Written as two sections, Banks wrote the lyrics as a political protest based on the idea that politicians often fail to think through the consequences of their actions. It's one of only two longer songs (ie more than five minutes) on *Invisible Touch*, which tended, at that time, as Mike Rutherford put it, "to be dwarfed by the power of television" as a result of the popularity of MTV videos.

Apart from 'Anything She Does' (based on captions for pornographic images) and the instrumental 'The Brazilian' (put together using various sounds programmed into Collins's new electronic drum kit), the remaining five tracks were all released as singles. All made it into the Top 5 in the US – the first group and foreign act to achieve it. Impressive, but that didn't keep a lot of diehard Genesis fans too happy. The album's subject matters were considered by many to be rather transparent, and the tunes pleasant but not particularly memorable. Whatever their opinions, when it came to voting with their cash, the album sold over 15 million copies worldwide.

Not surprisingly, the album was received with a very mixed reaction from critics upon release, several drawing comparisons with Phil Collins's solo work, or regretting the lack of input from Banks and Rutherford. "Could almost pass as outtakes from *No Jacket Required*," stated the *Chicago Tribune*. The AllMusic website agreed this was Genesis' poppiest album, "but still very definitely Genesis", they said. While *Ultimate Classic Rock* described it as "radio-ready piffle, replete with all the worst that '80s overproduction had to offer… just the tiniest bit of the 'old' Genesis is discernible in a couple of tracks."

'Tiniest' is better than none, but only just.

Released:
November 1991
Label:
Virgin/Atlantic
Producer:
Genesis and Nick Davis
Recorded:
Relight Studios, Hilvarenbeek, Netherlands
UK:
1
USA:
4

Tracks:

1. No Son of Mine
2. Jesus He Knows Me
3. Driving the Last Spike
4. I Can't Dance
5. Never a Time
6. Dreaming While You Sleep
7. Tell Me Why
8. Living Forever
9. Hold on My Heart
10. Way of the World
11. Since I Lost You
12. Fading Lights

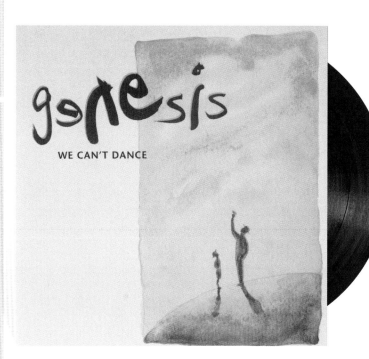

Perhaps somebody can explain to me why this penultimate Genesis album is so slated and disliked by so many? We've moved into the Nineties and, yes, it may in places sound more like a Phil Collins's solo LP (so did the previous three Genesis albums), but it says 'Genesis' on the front, and both Tony Banks and Mike Rutherford play on it and wrote some of the songs; yes, it's their most poppy LP so far but its production values are higher than several that swooped under the radar of criticism back in the Eighties. Ok, yes, there's that dreadful 'I Can't Dance' MTV video, but that's got nothing to do with the LP. All in all, it's a decent album. There, I've said it.

The band had spent almost four years concentrating on solo projects following the commercial success of 1986's *Invisible Touch* album and a 112-date follow-up

N'T DANCE

worldwide tour. By that point, Phil Collins's solo career had sky-rocketed, while Mike Rutherford's band, Mike and the Mechanics, were also enjoying reasonable success. Nevertheless, the band members were very keen to work together after such a long break and brought in a new producer/engineer, Nick Davis, who had worked on Banks's and Rutherford's solo material, to inject some new enthusiasm into the recording.

Although the original plan was for each band member to be allocated one third of lyric writing for the album, ultimately it was Phil Collins who wrote the majority, including several tracks on deeper, more serious issues than the band normally dealt with, including the opening 'No Son of Mine', a fine song on the subject of domestic abuse. 'Jesus He Knew Me' is better still, injecting an element of humour into the album on the topic of money grabbing, televangelist preachers in the USA, despite upsetting many American fans.

The 10-minute long 'Driving the Last Spike' was inspired by a book Phil had been given concerning 19th Century workers constructing the UK railway network – a nicely composed and performed number covering social history, which could easily have come from the mouths of Peter Gabriel or Sting. 'I Can't Dance' is a good old-fashioned rocker having a light dig at fashion models and which, with Jagger on vocals rather than Collins,

could easily be passed off as another hit for the Stones. 'Never a Time' is a straight broken-hearted ballad, while 'Dreaming While You Sleep' concerns the guilt of a hit and run driver, and 'Tell Me Why' criticises the Gulf War; all are respectable, soft-rock numbers that grow on you the more you listen. In fact, there's not a 'bad' song among the album's opening seven tracks. True, it does peak rather early and would have been improved overall by less material, especially fewer ballads; some of the remaining five tracks outstay their welcome, but this was produced as a CD, so there was plenty of time and space to play with after such a long layoff.

On release it was somewhat ironic that, while musically the album was considered by several critics to be outstanding, it was the band's attempts lyrically to work on more serious song subjects that took the most battering. Described by various newspapers as "soulless", "bland" and "obnoxious, over-produced pop pap" sounding like "castoffs" from one of Phil solo albums, it must have been hard to swallow at the time, but reaching the Top 5 in both the UK and US would have softened the blow.

Anyone who regards *We Can't Dance* as not so bad has to be prepared to take a battering as well. Batter away. I think it's one of Genesis' better Banks/Rutherford/Collins albums.

Released:
September 1997
Label:
Virgin/Atlantic
Producer:
Nick Davis, Tony Banks and Mike Rutherford
Recorded:
Relight Studios, Hilvarenbeek, Netherlands
UK:
2
USA:
54

Tracks:

1. Calling All Stations
2. Congo
3. Shipwrecked
4. Alien Afternoon
5. Not About Us
6. If That's What You Need
7. The Dividing Line
8. Uncertain Weather
9. Small Talk
10. There Must Be Some Other Way
11. One Man's Fool

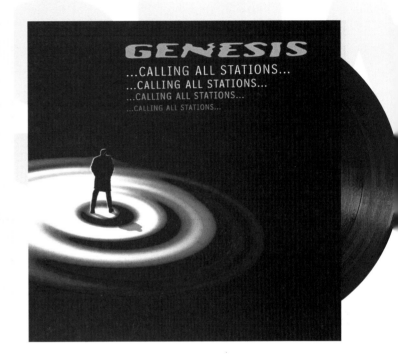

Having found positive things to say about some of the later Genesis albums that have been heavily criticised, you won't be surprised to discover that... we won't be doing that with this, the final Genesis studio album.

The band had been working on solo projects since the end of the 'We Can't Dance Tour' in 1992 and it was not until 1996 that Phil Collins officially left Genesis. The two remaining band members had a choice to make: call it a day, or stiff upper lip and carry on. Surprisingly, somewhat, it was Tony Banks who suggested the first option might be the most sensible, but Mike Rutherford persuaded him to come into the studio at the Farm in 1996 just to see what might happen. As always, long jamming sessions produced several interesting ideas but they still had to find a singer.

ING ALL
TIONS

There were two very strong candidates: from Nottingham, England, was the multi-instrumentalist David Longdon (now with Big Big Train); but it was Edinburgh-based Ray Wilson of the band Stiltskin, who'd had a UK No. 1 hit in 1994 with 'Inside', who was chosen for the role, with two session players – Israeli Nir Zidkyahu and American Nick D'Virgilio – to handle drums.

While Ray Wilson said that his input into the album was minimal, which is understandable, there's little doubt from the opening rock chords of the opening title track that this is more Stiltskin than Genesis. With his darker, edgier vocals, it kicks off with a decent soft-rock number that drifts into the softer still 'Congo' and 'Shipwrecked'; but 15 minutes in, you're pretty sure where this album is heading and it's not into Genesis territory.

On its release, the press on both sides of the Atlantic were far from kind. In a word, "inexplicable" said the *Guardian*, while the *Chicago Tribune* summed up Ray Wilson's performance as having "no confidence or personality, let alone the vision to stave off his bandmates' meandering ideas".

Harsh, and not entirely fair. Wilson has a great voice but was being asked to sing some pretty awful songs, several of which had already been written long before he arrived to record at the Farm, and just weren't right for him. Banks and Rutherford also struggled in terms of coming up with improvisational ideas – two people jamming is not a band. It needed that third catalyst and producer/engineer Nick Davis wasn't enough. None of the finished numbers really stand out and finding positives is not easy, but 'Calling All Stations' is a decent opener, while the closing 9-minute 'One Man's Fool' isn't bad either; its midway instrumental break leads into a 4-minute chorus finale that sounds, at times, uncannily like Oasis. Really! Probably the best part of the album.

All a bit of a shame, really. It would be 18 months before Ray would be told that there wouldn't be another Genesis album, which he wasn't too happy about but they departed as friends. As Ray commented: "The perfect gentlemen to work with. I learnt a lot and enjoyed it. I was looking forward to writing the next album together from the start."

The writing, unfortunately, was on the wall.

GENESIS' STU

From Worst To Best?

CALLING ALL STATIONS (1997)

And then there were two so they brought in Ray Wilson on vocals and two session drummers to replace Phil Collins, but sadly it just didn't work. Sounds less like Genesis than their 1969 debut album, and that's saying something.

FROM GENESIS TO REVELATION (1969)

Aspects of this album are surprisingly good for a bunch of teenage school kids left in the dubious hands of Jonathan King and his string arranger. Worth a listen but not likely to hog your turntable. Good effort, C-minus. See me later.

ABACAB (1981)

Hugh Padgham arrives in the sound engineers chair to help Genesis produce their own album, but then accidently reinvents drums and creates a monster that dominates the sound of the '80s. No tracks that standout apart from 'Who Dunnit', for all the wrong reasons.

GENESIS (1983)

Shorter, snappier songs are the answer for the band's second coming, hence the title, and they even have a go at a bit of rap with 'Mama', their first and only UK Top 5 hit. A good Side 1, but let down overall by Padgham's overproduction and the Side 2 turkey 'Illegal Alien'.

...AND THEN THERE WERE THREE... (1978)

Punk and new wave took over the UK music scene but failed in their attempt to wipe out dinosaurs for the second time in world history. The opening guitar riff on the aptly-titled 'Down and Out' sounds uncannily like the Sex Pistol's 'Pretty Vacant', but not a lot that's memorable until the last two tracks, 'The Lady Lies' and 'Follow You Follow Me'. That's the future.

INVISIBLE TOUCH (1986)

The US singles album, with five Top 5 hits – the first foreign performers to achieve that – although die-hard fans weren't overly impressed. Overproduced by Hugh Padgham once again but rescued by the almost 11-minutes 'Domino' to remind fans that there's still a semblance of prog-rockers in the old dogs yet.

WE CAN'T DANCE (1990)

 Has had to put up with a lot of criticism because of (in keeping with *Invisible Touch*) its similarities to Phil Collins's solo albums, but in reality is much better than most of the latter Banks/Rutherford/Collins releases. Some great songs and less of the dreaded gated-reverb drum bashing.

DUKE (1980)

A great album from a band on the threshold of their second giant step from proggers to popsters. They do it very well but with an inevitable result that hit singles became more important than a more cohesive album. The old Genesis concept, with one-side being the 'Duke' song suite, would have made it more interesting.

WIND & WUTHERING (1976)

Following less than a year after *A Trick of the Tail*, Steve Hackett was at his peak and this, his Genesis swansong, has much to commend it, particularly 'Blood on the Rooftops'. But Tony Banks dominates this album; more room for other writers could have improved fan-appreciation considerably.

NURSERY CRYME (1971)

A transitional album (it's Genesis – they all are!) but the opening conceptual piece 'The Musical Box' is the most obvious signpost as to where this band is heading. A terrific opening Side 1, but flip it over and the second lacks direction, tails off and fades away. Still, a better album than is often given credit for.

TRESPASS (1970)

A remarkable second album from a band still largely made up of recently graduated schoolboys. How they made the giant leap from recording their placid debut in 1968 to this in less than 22 months is remarkable. Genuine talent, two years' graft, and a great collection of songs, is all it took.

A TRICK OF THE TALE (1976)

Gabriel has departed and Genesis fans held their breath in anticipation of disappointment. What they got was one of the band's best Seventies albums with some terrific songs and Phil Collins's vocals sounding uncannily like Peter's. Things were going to be ok after all...

THE LAMB LIES DOWN ON BROADWAY (1974)

The classic difficult double album: completely in contrast to previous material and initially disliked by band members, fans and reviewers alike, but now recognised as a work of brilliance. Dominated by Peter Gabriel, its only flaw is that most of the best material is up front. Otherwise, this is a rollercoaster of an album.

SELLING ENGLAND BY THE POUND (1973)

Their poppiest early album, it drips of typically English, folky-pastoral ditties and amusing eccentricity. The majority of fans consider this to be the band's best ever, and it's easy to understand why. But, overall, is it perhaps a little lacking in energy and aggression in their attempt to rescue the diminishment of English culture?

FOXTROT (1973)

The top three Genesis albums from 1972-74 are all interchangeable, all are so good, their order of preference can change day by day depending on your mood or how much time you have to spare. But, overall, I believe, purely on the strength of 'Supper's Ready' alone (although Side 1 is pretty damn good, too), *Foxtrot* is the Genesis masterpiece.

A selection of the best compilations, boxsets, collections and live albums

GENESIS ARCHIVE: 1967-75 1998

Released in June 1998 on Virgin and Atlantic, the set includes previously unreleased studio, live, and demo tracks, including the first official live release of a full performance of *The Lamb Lies Down on Broadway*, recorded in 1975 at the Shrine Auditorium in Los Angeles. The remaining two CDs contain previously unreleased live tracks from 1973, demos and a BBC radio session from 1970. Comes with an 80-page booklet including interesting short articles written by Tony Banks, Jonathan King, *Melody Maker* journalist Chris Welch, tour manager Richard Macphail, the Friars Club in Aylesbury's promoter Dave Stopps, Charisma Records' US manager Ed Goodgold, and Charisma's founder Tony Stratton Smith.

TURN IT ON AGAIN: The Hits 1999/2007

Originally released as a single album by Virgin in the UK and Atlantic in the US but, in 2007, an expanded two-disc, *The Tour Edition*, was released to promote the 'Turn It on Again: The Tour'. Both versions made it into the Top 5 in the UK. The 2007 version features songs from every studio album except *Foxtrot* and *From Genesis to Revelation*. A 2-CD/2-DVD version was also issued with *The Video Show* and *When in Rome 2007* DVDs.

GENESIS ARCHIVE 2: 1976-1992 2000

Three discs of mainly unreleased live recordings, some B-sides and remixes plus tracks from the *Spot the Pigeon* and *3X3* EPs, all from the Banks-Rutherford-Collins era apart from four songs that also feature Steve Hackett. Chester Thompson, Daryl Stuermer and Bill Bruford appear on various live tracks.

PLATINUM COLLECTION 2004

Their most comprehensive, career-spanning, 3-CD boxset covering every studio album apart from *From Genesis to Revelation*, which is a shame but the band no longer owned the rights to that material. The majority of tracks have been remixed by co-producer and engineer Nick Davis. Reached 21 in the UK charts.

GENESIS 1976-1982 2007

The first of three excellent Genesis boxsets released by Virgin/EMI in Europe and Japan, and by Atlantic/Rhino in the US and Canada. This first release features five albums from *A Trick of the Tail* to *Abacab*. All three sets offer digitally re-mastered studio albums on CD with additional DVDs including audio versions in 5.1 surround sound mixes in DTS and Dolby Stereo, engineered by Nick Davis. In the Virgin/EMI versions for Europe and Japan, the CDs are hybrid Super Audio CD (SACD)/CDs. The DVDs include a selection of videos of songs from the album, Genesis documentaries, live performances, band member interviews and various photo galleries of tour programmes etc.

Each of the three sets also includes a pair of two Extra Tracks CDs/DVDs; this 1976-1982 set features various B-sides and tracks from the *Spot the Pigeon* EP, as well as a CD booklet including articles written by road manager Richard Macphail and celebrity Genesis fans – comedian David Baddiel, Queen's drummer Roger Taylor, TV presenter Jeremy Clarkson and actor Tony Robinson, from *Black Adder*. (In 2012, a 5LP 180g vinyl version of this boxset was issued in the UK.)

GENESIS 1983-1998 2007

The second release of the CD/DVD boxsets of four Genesis studio albums from *Genesis* to *Calling All Stations*. The fifth pair of discs of Extra Tracks includes B-sides, and three tracks from the *Not About Us* 4-track CD released in 1998, plus live performances at Knebworth in 1993 and the Music Managers Forum Awards Ceremony in 2000. (In 2015, a 6LP 180g vinyl version of this boxset was issued in the UK.)

GENESIS 1970-1975 2008

The third release of the CD/DVD boxsets of the first five studio albums from *Trespass* to *The Lamb Lies Down on Broadway*. The sixth pair of discs of Extra Tracks includes B-sides, three rare songs from BBC Sessions for the 'Night Ride' radio show in 1970 and the *Genesis Plays Jackson* soundtrack which has never been released before. (In 2008 a limited edition 6LP 180g vinyl version of this boxset was issued in the UK.)

R-KIVE 2014

Another 3-CD career-spanning boxset as a companion to the BBC documentary *Genesis: Together and Apart*, which, interestingly, also features solo releases as well as tracks from every Genesis studio album except *From Genesis to Revelation*. Solo material includes Peter Gabriel's 'Solsbury Hill' and 'Biko'; Tony Banks's 'For a While'; Mike and the Mechanics' 'The Living Years' and 'Over My Shoulder'; Steve Hackett's 'Every Day' and 'Nomads'; and Phil Collins's 'In the Air Tonight' and 'Easy Lover'. The BBC documentary was released in October 2014 on DVD under the title *Genesis: Sum of the Parts*.

50 YEARS AGO 2017

An album released by Jonathan King's Jonjo Music (for download only) featuring early Genesis recordings from *From Genesis to Revelation* said to have been unearthed in an old warehouse following the sale of London's Regent Sounds Studio in the Seventies. The tapes were forwarded to King who has (with Steve Levine) remixed the tracks – some as new stereo mixes, some featuring the band's vocals without any instrumentation, and some without his cloying string arrangements.

THE LAST DOMINO? 2021

A recent compilation celebrating the return of Genesis for their 2021/22 arena world tour, collecting together the band's many well-known hits along with album selections from across their 50-year-plus career. Available as a double CD or 4LP boxset – the first time a career-encompassing Genesis collection has been made available on heavyweight vinyl housed in a hardback gatefold cover sleeve.

REFUGEES: An Anthology Of The Famous Charisma Label 1969–1978 2009

A terrific 3-CD collection released by Virgin Records which includes three Genesis numbers – 'Looking for Someone', 'Twilight Alehouse' and 'Match of the Day' – plus an interesting choice of material from their important label mates in the band's earlier days, including solo songs from Steve Hackett and Peter Gabriel, two tracks from Phil Collins's Brand X, and excellent choices from bands such as Rare Bird, Van Der Graaf Generator, Lindisfarne, the Nice, Monty Python and many others.

THE FAMOUS CHARISMA BOX: The History Of Charisma Records 1968–1985 1993

This earlier 4-CD boxset was released by Virgin in 1993 and features an even more eclectic choice of Charisma performers including Vivian Stanshall, Barry Humphries and Sir John Betjeman, but with two Genesis numbers – 'The Knife' and 'Happy the Man' – plus additional solo material from Mike Rutherford and Tony Banks.

THE CHARISMA POSER: A Potted History Of Charisma Records 1993

This single disc version using *The Famous Charisma Box* cover was released in the same year with 18 tracks including 'Afterglow' from Genesis.

CHARISMA DISTURBANCE 1973

The first of two Charisma collections on vinyl, neither of which are too difficult to find. This double album sampler includes Genesis' 'Return of the Giant Hogweed'.

ONE MORE CHANCE 1974

Single LP including one track from Genesis, 'Happy the Man'.

GENESIS LIVE 1973

Recorded live in Manchester and Leicester in 1973, originally as a live radio broadcast for America, it was subsequently withheld from the US as the recording quality was considered unacceptable. To save face, it was released as a budget live LP by Charisma for sale in UK mass-market retail outlets and made it to No. 9 in the UK charts. Despite the poor sound quality on vinyl, it's a decent recording of five of Genesis' best longer pieces taken from *Trespass*, *Nursery Cryme* and *Foxtrot*. A remastered version was released on CD in 1994 by Virgin Records in the UK and Atlantic in the US. The rear cover includes Peter Gabriel's short story that was seen by the film director William Friedkin (*The Exorcist*) and resulted in Gabriel being invited to Hollywood to discuss contributions to ideas for film scripts.

SECONDS OUT 1977

Their second live album, a double LP from Charisma recorded in two locations in Paris, France, between 1976-77, hence no Peter Gabriel and released in October '77 two months after Steve Hackett's departure. A terrific live recording that surprised many on hearing the quality of Phil Collins's vocals and the standard of drumming from newly recruited Chester Thompson sharing the drum stool with Collins. Offering an interesting selection of numbers from *Nursery Cryme* through to *Wind & Wuthering*, including Side 3 devoted to the magnificent 'Supper's Ready', this is generally considered the best live Genesis album. Sold reasonably well, reaching No. 4 in the UK and No. 47 in the US.

THREE SIDES LIVE 1982

Third live double LP released in 1982 by Charisma. The first three sides on the UK version feature songs primarily from their 1981 tour, with the addition of 'Follow You, Follow Me' at the Lyceum Theatre in London in 1980. Side 4 is made up of three live UK recordings from 1976, '78 and '80, including 'Fountain at Salmacis' at Knebworth Festival. A decent live album throughout which reached No. 2 in the UK, although lacking some of the energy *Seconds Out* provided. The puzzling title of only *Three Sides Live* comes from the fact that on the US version, released by Atlantic and making it to No. 10 in the charts, the fourth side features studio recordings from the band's second EP *3x3* and the B-sides of two singles.

THE WAY WE WALK, VOLUME 1: The Shorts 1992

Live album number four released by Virgin Records in the UK and Atlantic in the USA. A compilation of recordings from their 1986–1987 'Invisible Touch Tour' and 1992 'We Can't Dance Tour' focussing on their radio-friendly hit singles. Reached No. 3 in the UK and No. 35 in the US.

THE WAY WE WALK, VOLUME 2: The Longs 1993

The fifth live album is the companion to the above, recorded during their 1992 'We Can't Dance Tour'. Fairly obviously, Volume 2 concentrates on the longer songs performed during this period plus a revised medley of older songs ('Dance on a Volcano'/'The Lamb Lies Down on Broadway'/'The Musical Box'/'Firth of Fifth'/'I Know What I Like [In Your Wardrobe])'. Made it to the top in the UK charts – the last ever Genesis No. 1 album; reached No. 20 in the US.

LIVE OVER EUROPE 2007 2007

The band's sixth official live album recorded during the 'Turn it on Again: The Tour' at various European locations in the UK, France, Netherlands, Germany, Italy, Finland and the Czech Republic. Produced by Nick Davis as a companion disc for the *When in Rome 2007* DVD featuring a live performance in front of an estimated half-a-million fans.

GENESIS KNEBWORTH 1978: A Midsummer Night's Dream 2007

A BBC FM recording taken direct from the soundboard at Knebworth Festival in June '78, in front of an estimated 150,000 fans. A terrific performance and with much better quality sound than many of the other poor, bootleg-quality Knebworth recordings from over the years. Not too difficult to find online.

GENESIS LIVE 1973–2007 2009

This live album collection comes in the same smart format as the studio album boxsets released in 2007-08. Includes the live albums *Genesis Live, Seconds Out,* and *Live at the Rainbow 1973,* all with bonus DVDs that feature the albums in 5.1 surround sound. *Three Sides Live* and *The Way We Walk* (Volumes 1 and 2) are included on stereo CDs only. *Live Over Europe 2007* is not included in the boxset but an empty slot is provided for those who wish to add it to the collection.

GENESIS THE MOVIE BOX 1981–2007 2009

Also in the same format as the *Genesis Live 1973-2007,* this collection includes DVDs of four Genesis films - *Three Sides Live* (1981), *The Mama Tour* (1984), *Live at Wembley Stadium* (1987) and *The Way We Walk - Live in Concert* (1992), plus a bonus disc which includes an updated version of the *Behind The Music* documentary originally broadcast in 1999. As with the studio album boxsets, all contain new 5.1 surround sound mixes in DTS and Dolby Digital. The *When in Rome Live* is not included in the boxset but an empty slot is provided for those who wish to add it to the collection.

LIVE AT KNEBWORTH 2021

Genesis released *Live At Knebworth* through Mercury Studios for the 2021 Record Store Day. Recorded on June 30 1990, this limited edition vinyl EP features 'Mama' and the band's 'Turn It On Again' medley, featuring excerpts of Sixties classics such as: 'Somebody to Love', '(I Can't Get No) Satisfaction', 'Twist And Shout', 'Reach Out I'll Be There', 'You've Lost That Lovin' Feeling', 'Pinball Wizard' and 'In the Midnight Hour'. All artists performed for free to raise money for Nordoff-Robbins Music Therapy and the Brit School for Performing Arts.